THE TREE AND
THE Master

THE TREE AND THE Master ❧

AN ANTHOLOGY OF LITERATURE ON THE CROSS OF Christ

EDITED BY

Sister Mary Immaculate

OF THE CONGREGATION OF THE SISTERS OF THE HOLY CROSS

Preface by W. H. Auden

New York Random House

FIRST PRINTING

© Copyright, 1965, by *Sister Mary Immaculate*, C.S.C.
All rights reserved under International and Pan-
American Copyright Conventions. Published in
New York by Random House, Inc., and simul-
taneously in Toronto, Canada, by Random House
of Canada Limited.

Library of Congress Catalog Card Number: 65-11263

Manufactured in the United States of America
by The Haddon Craftsmen, Scranton, Pa.

ACKNOWLEDGMENTS

The editor thanks the following authors, their translators, publishers, and agents for permission to include copyrighted material in this anthology:

THE AMERICA PRESS, for the selection from "The Mental Sufferings of Our Lord in His Passion" by John Henry Cardinal Newman from *Favorite Newman Sermons,* edited by Daniel M. O'Connell, S. J., copyright, 1940, by The America Press.

THE AMERICAN-SCANDINAVIAN FOUNDATION, for "Man Carries Woman" by Tore Örjassaeter in *Anthology of Norwegian Lyrics,* translated by Charles Wharton Stork, published by Princeton University Press, copyright, 1940, by The American-Scandinavian Foundation; for "The Holy Eucharist" by Adam Oehlenschläger, translated by S. Foster Damon and Robert S. Hillyer, published by Oxford University Press, copyright, 1922, by The American-Scandinavian Foundation.

JAMES BENÉT, for permission acknowledged under The Dial Press.

BENZIGER BROTHERS, INC., for the selections from the *Summa Theologica* by St. Thomas Aquinas, translated by Fathers of the English Dominican Province, copyright, 1947, by Benziger Brothers, Inc.

DAS BERGLAND-BUCH, Salzburg, for translation rights for "Gethsemane" from *Werke* by Annette von Dröste Hülshoff, edited by Joseph Köselschen, copyright, 1963, by Das Bergland-Buch.

GEOFFREY BLES, LTD., for permissions acknowledged under The Macmillan Company.

CURTIS BROWN, LTD., for permission acknowledged under Random House, Inc.

THE BRUCE PUBLISHING COMPANY, for the selection from "Of the Royal Road of the Holy Cross" from *The Imitation of Christ* by Thomas à Kempis, translated by Aloysius Croft and Harold Bolton, copyright, 1948, by The Bruce Publishing Company.

BURNS AND OATES, LTD., for "The Crucifixion" by Alice Meynell from *Collected Poems,* copyright, 1940, by Burns and Oates, Ltd.; for permissions acknowledged under Harper and Row, The Newman Press, and Random House, Inc.

JONATHAN CAPE, LTD., for permission acknowledged under Holt, Rinehart and Winston, Inc.

GEOFFREY CHAPMAN, LTD., for the selection from *Christian Humanism* by Louis Boyer, copyright, 1959, by Geoffrey Chapman, Ltd.; for permissions acknowledged under Sheed and Ward, Inc.

CHATTO AND WINDUS, LTD., for permission acknowledged under Random House, Inc.

CHILMARK PRESS, for the selection from *The Anathémata* by David Jones, copyright, 1963, by Chilmark Press, reprinted by permission of Chilmark Press and David Jones.

WILLIAM COLLINS AND SONS, for permissions acknowledged under Harper and Row, and Sheed and Ward, Inc.

THE COMMONWEAL, for "Pastorale" by Lopé de Vega, English version taken from the Spanish by Sister Mary Immaculate, C.S.C., copyright, 1943, by *The Commonweal.*

CONSTABLE AND COMPANY, LTD., for "The Word of the Cross" by Paulinus of Nola; for "Easter Sunday" by Sedulius Scottus; for "Good Friday: the Third Nocturne" by Peter Abelard; for "The Virgin Martyrs" by Sigebert of Gembloux, all four poems translated from the Latin by Helen Waddell, published by Henry Holt and Company, copyright, 1942, by Constable and Company, Ltd.; for "The Crucifixion" translated by Kuno Meyer, from *The Oxford Book of Irish Verse,* published by Oxford University Press, New York, 1958, copyright, 1958, by Constable and Company, Ltd.

DORIS DANA AND JOAN DAVES, for permission to translate from the Spanish "Nocturno del Descendimiento" by Gabriela Mistral from *Poesias Completas,* Premino Nobel Edición, published by Aguilar, Madrid, copyright, 1945, by Aguilar, Madrid.

J. M. DENT AND SONS, LTD., for permissions acknowledged under E. P. Dutton and Company, Inc., and New Directions.

THE DEVIN-ADAIR COMPANY, for the selection from *It All Goes Together* by Eric Gill, copyright, 1944, by The Devin-Adair Company.

THE DIAL PRESS, for "The Galilean" from "The Dust Which is God" by William Rose Benét from *This is My Best,* edited by Whit Burnett, copyright, 1942, by The Dial Press, reprinted by permission of James Benét.

DODD, MEAD AND COMPANY, for the selection from *Orthodoxy* by G. K. Chesterton, copyright, 1940.

DOUBLEDAY AND COMPANY, INC., for the selection from *The Greatest Story Ever Told* by Fulton Oursler, copyright, 1949, by Fulton Oursler, reprinted by permission of Doubleday and Company, Inc.; for "The Huckster" from *Requiem,* published by Doubleday, Doran and Company, 1928, copyright, 1927, by Humbert Wolfe, reprinted by permission of Ann Wolfe.

RONALD DUNCAN, for the selection from *Judas,* by Ronald Duncan, published in limited edition by Anthony Bond, Ltd., copyright, 1960, by Anthony Bond, Ltd.

E. P. DUTTON AND COMPANY, INC., for the selection from *Essays and Addresses on the Philosophy of Religion* by Friederich von Hügel, copyright, 1927, by E. P. Dutton and Company, Inc., reprinted by permission also of J. M. Dent and Sons, Ltd.

EDITIONS GALLIMARD, for permissions acknowledged under Holt, Rinehart and Winston, Inc., and Henry Regnery Company.

EYRE AND SPOTTISWOODE, for permission acknowledged under Charles Scribner's Sons.

FABER AND FABER, LTD., for "Place of a Skull" from *Holes in the Sky* by Louis MacNeice, copyright, 1949, by Faber and Faber, Ltd.; for "The Crucifix" by Alexander Pushkin from *Poems from the Russian,* translated by Frances Cornford and E. P. Salaman, copyright, 1943, by Faber and Faber, Ltd.; for permissions acknowledged under Farrar, Straus and Company, Grove Press, Inc., and New Directions.

FARRAR, STRAUS AND COMPANY, INC., for the selection from *The Violent Bear It Away* by Flannery O'Connor, copyright © 1955, 1960, by Flannery O'Connor, reprinted by permission also of Longmans, Green and Company, Ltd., London; for the selection from "Canticle of Darkness" from *Friday's Child* by Wilfred Watson, copyright, 1955, by Wilfred Watson.

GINN AND COMPANY, for "He Bare Him Up," anonymous, from *A Literary Middle English Reader* edited by A. S. Cook, published by the Blaisdell Publishing Company, copyright, 1915, by Ginn and Company.

FRIDA GROSSER, for her translations from the German: "At Daybreak" by Hugo von Hofmannsthal; "Gethsemane" by Annette von Dröste Hülshoff; "A Spiritual Song" by Georg Trakl.

GROVE PRESS, INC., for "Monologue for the Good Friday Christ" in *Cycle for Mother Cabrini* by John Logan, copyright, 1955, by John Logan, reprinted by permission of John Logan; for "The Killing" from *Collected Poems* by Edwin Muir, copyright, 1957, by Edwin Muir, reprinted by permission also of Faber and Faber, Ltd.; for "Madrigal a lo divino: Of Christ and the Soul" from *The Poems of St. John of the Cross, New English Versions* by John Frederick Nims, copyright, 1959, by John Frederick Nims.

HARCOURT, BRACE, AND WORLD, INC., for "The Crucifix" from *Lord Weary's Castle* by Robert Lowell, copyright, 1944, 1946, by Robert Lowell, reprinted by permission of Harcourt, Brace, and World, Inc.; for the selection from "East Coker" in *Four Quartets* by T. S. Eliot, copyright, 1943, by T. S. Eliot, reprinted by permission of Harcourt, Brace, and World, Inc. and T. S. Eliot; for the selection from "Passion in the Andes" in *Collected*

Edition of Heywood Broun, edited by Heywood Hale Broun, copyright, 1939 and 1941, by Heywood Hale Broun, reprinted by permission of Heywood Hale Broun and Constance Broun.

HARPER AND ROW, PUBLISHERS, INC., for the selection from *The Divine Milieu* by Pierre Teilhard de Chardin, copyright, 1960, by Harper and Row, Inc., reprinted by permission also of William Collins and Sons; for the selections from *Greek Myths and Christian Mystery* by Hugo Rahner, copyright, 1963, by Harper and Row, Inc., reprinted by permission also of Burns and Oates, Ltd.; for the selection from *Revelations of Divine* Love by Juliana of Norwich, translated by James Walsh, S.J., copyright, 1962, by Harper and Row, Inc., reprinted by permission also of Burns and Oates, Ltd.; for the selection from *Dogmatics in Outline* by Karl Barth from the Harper Torchbooks, copyright, 1959, by Harper and Row, Inc., reprinted by permission also of Student Christian Movement Press, Ltd.; for "The Little Hill" by Edna St. Vincent Millay, from *Collected Lyrics,* copyright, 1921, 1948, by Edna St. Vincent Millay, reprinted by permission of Norma Millay Ellis.

HARVARD UNIVERSITY PRESS, THE BELKNAP PRESS, for "Jesus! Thy Crucifix" by Emily Dickinson from *The Poems of Emily Dickinson,* edited by Thomas H. Johnson, copyright, 1951, 1955, by the President and Fellows of Harvard College, reprinted by permission of the publishers and the trustees of Amherst College.

WILLIAM HEINEMAN LTD., for permission acknowledged under William Morrow.

B. HERDER COMPANY, for the selection from *The Cross of Jesus* by Louis Chardon, copyright, 1957, by B. Herder Company.

DAVID HIGHAM ASSOCIATES, LTD., for permission acknowledged under Vanguard Press.

HOLT, RINEHART AND WINSTON, INC., for "Easter Hymn" from *Complete Poems* by A. E. Housman, copyright, 1936, by Barclays Bank Ltd., copyright renewed © 1964, by Robert E. Symons, reprinted by permission of Holt, Rinehart and Winston, Inc., and also by permission of the Society of Authors and Messrs. Jonathan Cape Ltd., publishers of A. E. Housman's *Collected Poems*; for "Easter Day" from *I Believe in God* by Paul Claudel, edited by Agnes du Sarment, translated by Helen Weaver, copyright © 1961, by Librairie Gallimard, translation copyright © 1963, by Holt, Rinehart and Winston, Inc., reprinted by permission of Holt, Rinehart and Winston, Inc.

HOUGHTON MIFFLIN COMPANY, for the selection from *Troilus and Criseyde* by Geoffrey Chaucer from *The Works of Geoffrey Chaucer,* edited by F. N. Robinson, copyright, 1957, by Houghton Mifflin Company; for "Eve's First Prophecy" from *Songs for Eve* by Archibald Macleish, copyright, 1954, by Houghton Mifflin Company; for "With Mercy for the Greedy" from *All My Pretty Ones* by Anne Sexton, copyright, 1962, by Houghton Mifflin Company, reprinted by permission also of *Partisan Review.*

INSEL-BÜCHEREI 461, Frankfurt, for permission to translate "Vor Tag" by Hugo Hofmannsthal from his *Gedichte,* copyright, 1957, by Insel-Bücherei.

THE JOHNS HOPKINS PRESS, for "Rose" from *The Christ of Velázquez* by Miguel de Unamuno, translated by Eleanor L. Turnbull, copyright, 1951, by The Johns Hopkins Press.

ALFRED A. KNOPF, INC., for the selection from *Kristin Lavransdatter* by Sigrid Undset, translated by Charles Archer, copyright, 1946, by Alfred A. Knopf, Inc., reprinted by permission of Alfred A. Knopf, Inc.

JOHN LANE THE BODLEY HEAD LTD., for "Confession" by Anna Akhmatova, for "When Mountain-ash in Clusters Reddens" by Alexander Blok, for "Stigmata" by Maximilian Voloshin, all from *Modern Russian Poetry,* edited and translated by Babette Deutsch and Avrahm Yarmolinsky, copyright, 1923, by John Lane the Bodley Head Ltd.

LIBRAIRIE PLON, 8 Rue Garancière, Paris, for permissions acknowledged under The Macmillan Company.

LONGMANS, GREEN, New York, for permissions acknowledged under David McKay Company, Inc.

LONGMANS, GREEN AND COMPANY, LTD., London, for permissions acknowledged under Farrar, Straus and Company, Inc.

ISABEL GARCÍA LORCA, for permission to translate "Saeta" by Federico García Lorca, from *Obras Completas,* Aguilar, Madrid, copyright, 1955, by Aguilar.

THE MACMILLAN COMPANY, for the selection from *Diary of a Country Priest* by Georges Bernanos, copyright, 1954, by The Macmillan Company, reprinted by permission of The Macmillan Company and also of Librairie Plon, 8 Rue Garancière, Paris; for the selection from *The Incarnation of the Word* by St. Athanasius, copyright, 1951, by The Macmillan Company, reprinted by permission of The Macmillan Company and also of Geoffrey Bles, Ltd.; for "The Road to Emmaus" by Vyacheslav Ivanov in *A Book of Russian Verse,* translated by C. Maurice Bowra, copyright, 1941, by The Macmillan Company, London, reprinted by permission of St Martin's Press, Inc. and also by permission of C. Maurice Bowra.

MRS. NAOMI MATTHEWS, for permission acknowledged under University of Florida Press.

DAVID MCKAY COMPANY, INC., for the selection from *The Golden Legend* by Jacobus de Voragine, published by Longmans, Green and Company, New York, copyright, 1941, by Longmans, Green and Company, reprinted by courtesy of David McKay Company, Inc.; for the selection from *Adventures in Grace* by Raïssa Maritain, published by Longmans, Green and Company, New York, copyright, 1945, by Longmans, Green and Company, reprinted by courtesy of David McKay Company, Inc.

WILLIAM MORROW AND COMPANY, INC., for the selection from *The Devil's Advocate* by Morris L. West, copyright, 1959, by Morris L. West, reprinted also by permission of William Heinemann Ltd.

OTTO MÜLLER VERLAG, Salzburg, for permission to translate "Geistliches Lied" by Georg Trakl, from *Ergriffenes Dasein,* edited by Hans Egon Holthusen and Friedhelm Kemp, Langewiesche-Brandt, copyright, 1957, by Otto Müller Verlag.

NEW DIRECTIONS, for "The Ballad of the Goodly Fere" from *Personae* from *The Collected Poems of Ezra Pound,* copyright, 1924, 1926, by Ezra Pound, reprinted by permission of New Directions; for the selection from "Vision and Prayer" by Dylan Thomas, from *The Collected Poems of Dylan Thomas,* copyright ©, 1957, by New Directions, reprinted by permission of New Directions and also of J. M. Dent and Sons, Ltd.; for "An Argument of the Passion of Christ" from *A Man in a Divided Sea* by Thomas Merton, copyright, 1946, by New Directions, reprinted by permission of New Directions; for "Quem Quaeritis" from *Affinities* by Vernon Watkins, copyright, 1962, by Vernon Watkins, reprinted by permission of New Directions and by permission also of Faber and Faber, Ltd.

THE NEWMAN PRESS, for the selection from *The Little Flowers of St. Francis,* edited by Dom Roger Hudleston, O.S.B., copyright, 1952, by The Newman Press; for the selection from *The Love of God* by St. Francis de Sales, edited by Vincent Kerns, copyright, 1962, by The Newman Press; for the selection from *The Exercises of St. Gertrude,* edited by a Benedictine Nun of Regina Laudis Monastery, copyright, 1956, by The Newman Press, reprinted by permission also of Burns and Oates, Ltd.; for the selection from *Revelations of Divine Love* by St. Juliana of Norwich, edited by Dom Roger Hudleston, O.S.B., copyright, 1952, by The Newman Press, reprinted by permission also of Burns and Oates, Ltd.

NICHOLSON AND WATSON, LTD., for "Ecce Homo" by David Gascoyne, from *Poems, 1937-1942,* copyright, 1944, by Nicholson and Watson, Ltd.

NORTHWESTERN UNIVERSITY PRESS, for three poems from *"Théorèmes Spirituels"* by Jean de la Ceppède, translated by Clinton Larson in *Renaissance and Baroque Lyrics,* edited by Harold Martin Priest, copyright ©, 1962, by Northwestern University Press.

W. W. NORTON AND COMPANY, INC., for "The Last Supper" and "Pietà" by Rainer Maria Rilke, translated by M. D. Herter Norton in *Translations from the Poetry of Rainer Maria Rilke,* copyright, 1938, by W. W. Norton and Company, Inc.

ODYSSEY PRESS, INC., for the selection from *Paradise Lost* by John Milton, from *Complete Poems and Major Prose of John Milton,* edited by Merritt Y. Hughes, copyright, 1957, by the Odyssey Press, Inc.

OXFORD UNIVERSITY PRESS, New York, for the selection from *Thor, With Angels* by Christopher Fry, copyright, 1957, by Oxford University Press; for the selections from the "Elena" by Cynewulf, and for the anonymous "Dream of the Rood," both translated by Charles W. Kennedy in *Early English Christian Poetry,* copyright, 1960, by Oxford University Press; for the selection from *Theology of Culture* by Paul Tillich, edited by Robert C. Kimball, copyright, 1959, by Oxford University Press; for "In Holy Week" from *In the Interlude* by Boris Pasternak, translated by Henry Kamen, copyright ©, 1962, by Henry Kamen; for "Barnfloor and Winepress" from *Poems of Gerard Manley Hopkins,* edited by W. H. Gardner, copyright, 1948, by Oxford University Press; for "The Crucifixion" translated from the Irish by Kuno Meyer in *The Oxford Book of Irish Verse,* edited by D. MacDonaugh and Lennox Robinson, copyright, 1958, by Constable and Company, reprinted by permission of Constable and Company.

OXFORD, CLARENDON PRESS, for "Sunset on Calvary," from *English Lyrics of the Thirteenth Century,* edited by Carleton Brown, copyright, 1932, by the Clarendon Press.

PANTHEON BOOKS, INC., for permissions acknowledged under Random House, Inc.

PARTISAN REVIEW, for permission acknowledged under Houghton, Mifflin Company.

POETRY magazine, for "Rainbow," a translation from the French of Max Jacob by Elizabeth Bishop, copyright, 1950, by *Poetry,* and 1963 by Elizabeth Bishop, reprinted by permission of Elizabeth Bishop; for "Girls Going to Church" by John Ciardi, copyright, 1943, by *Poetry,* and 1963 by John Ciardi, reprinted by permission of John Ciardi; for "Bull" from *The Christ of Velázquez* by Miguel de Unamuno, and translated by Anthony Kerrigan, copyright, 1963, by *Poetry* and by Anthony Kerrigan, reprinted by permission of Anthony Kerrigan.

PRINCETON UNIVERSITY PRESS, for "Flower, Tree, and Bird" by Hermann Hesse from *Twentieth Century German Verse* edited by Herman Salinger, copyright, 1952, by Princeton University Press; for the selection from *Philosophical Fragments* by Sören Kierkegaard, copyright, 1962, by Princeton University Press; for permission acknowledged under American-Scandinavian Foundation.

G. P. PUTNAM'S SONS, for the selection from *Waiting for God* by Simone Weil, copyright, 1951, by G. P. Putnam's Sons.

PUTNAM'S AND COWARD-McCANN, for the selection "Easter: The Challenge to Death" from *Cain, Where Is Your Brother* by François Mauriac, copyright, 1962, by Putnam's and Coward-McCann.

KATHLEEN RAINE, for "Lenten Flowers" from *Collected Poems of Kathleen Raine,* published by Random House, New York, also by Hamish Hamilton Ltd., London, and by William Collins and Company, Ltd., Toronto; copyright, 1956, by Kathleen Raine.

RANDOM HOUSE, INC., for the selection from Gregory of Nyssa in *The Soul Afire,* edited by H. H. Reinhold, copyright, 1944, by Pantheon Books, Inc., reprinted by permission of Random House, Inc., and also by permission of Burns and Oates Ltd.; for the selection from *Barabbas* by Pär Lagerkvist, copyright, 1951, by Random House, Inc., reprinted by permission of Random House, Inc., and also by permission of Chatto and Windus, Ltd., London; for the selection from *The Sound and the Fury* by William Faulkner, copyright, 1929, renewed 1956, by William Faulkner, reprinted by permission of Random House, Inc., and also by permission of Curtis Brown, Ltd., London; for the selection from *The Mystery of the Charity of Joan of Arc* by Charles Péguy, translated by Julian Green, copyright, 1950, by Pantheon Books, Inc., reprinted by permission of Random House, Inc.; for the selection from *The Pilgrim of the Absolute* by Leon Bloy, translated by John Coleman and Henry L. Binsse, copyright, 1947, by Pantheon Books, Inc., reprinted by permission of Random House, Inc.; for the selection from *Pensées* by Blaise Pascal, translated by A. J. Denomy,

C.S.B., from *The Wisdom of Catholicism,* edited by Anton C. Pegis, copyright, 1949, by Random House, Inc.

HENRY REGNERY COMPANY, for the selection from *A Poet Before the Cross* by Paul Claudel, copyright, 1958, by Henry Regnery Company, by permission also of Editions Gallimard.

RUTGERS UNIVERSITY PRESS, for the anonymous poem "The Nightingale" and for "Mary at Canne" by Jan Engelman from *Coming After: An Anthology of Poetry from the Low Countries,* translated by Adriaan J. Barnouw, copyright, 1948, by Rutgers University Press.

ST MARTIN'S PRESS, INC., for "The Stair" from *The World's One Clock* by Louise Townsend Nicholl, copyright, 1959, by Louise Townsend Nicholl.

CHARLES SCRIBNER'S SONS, for "The Cross" by Allen Tate from *Poems 1922-1947* by Allen Tate, copyright, 1948, by Charles Scribner's Sons, reprinted by permission of Charles Scribner's Sons, and also by permission of Eyre and Spottiswood, Ltd.; for the selection from *Ransoming the Time* by Jacques Maritain, copyright, 1941, by Charles Scribner's Sons, reprinted by permission of Charles Scribner's Sons.

SHEED AND WARD, INC., for the selection from *Prayer* by Hans Urs von Balthasar, © 1961, by Geoffrey Chapman, Ltd., published by Sheed and Ward, Inc., New York; for the selections by Père Philippe de la Trinité and Gustave Thibon from *Love* and *Violence,* edited by P. Bruno de Jesus-Marie, O.D.C., copyright, 1954, by Sheed and Ward, Inc., New York, and reprinted by permission also of Sheed and Ward Ltd., London; for the selection from *St. Brigid of Ireland* by Alice Curtayne, copyright, 1954, by Sheed and Ward, Inc., New York; for the selection from *Christ and Us,* the English translation of *Approches du Christ* by Jean Daniélou, © A. R. Mowbray Ltd., 1961, published in U.S.A. by Sheed and Ward, Inc., New York; for the selection from *The Resurrection* by Francis X. Durrwell, © Sheed and Ward Ltd., 1960, published in U.S.A. by Sheed and Ward, Inc., New York; for "Easter" from *Hymns to the Church* by Gertrude von le Fort, copyright, 1953, by Sheed and Ward, Inc., New York; for the selection from *Life in Christ* by Julius Tyciak, copyright, 1937, by Sheed and Ward, Inc., New York, and reprinted by permission also of Sheed and Ward Ltd., London; for the selection from *The High Green Hill* by Gerald Vann, O.P., copyright, 1951, by Sheed and Ward, Inc., New York, and reprinted by permission also of William Collins and Sons, London; for the selection from *The Catholic Centre* by E. I. Watkin, copyright, 1939, by Sheed and Ward, Inc., New York, reprinted by permission also of Sheed and Ward Ltd., London; for the selection from *The Splendor of the Liturgy* by Maurice Zundel, copyright, 1939, by Sheed and Ward, Inc., New York, reprinted by permission also of Sheed and Ward Ltd., London.

SHEED AND WARD, LTD., London, for the selection from *The Dialogue of Comfort Against Tribulation* by St. Thomas More, copyright, 1951, by Sheed and Ward, Ltd., London; for several permissions acknowledged under Sheed and Ward, Inc., New York.

SISTER M. KATHARINE ELAINE, C.S.C., for her translations from the Spanish: "Magdalen Speaks" by Juan del Encina; "Nocturne of the Descent" by Gabriela Mistral; "Saeta" by Federico García Lorca; "To Jesus Crucified," anonymous, 16th century.

SISTER M. MARGARET DENYSE, C.S.C., for her translation, "The Crucifix," from the French of Alphonse de Lamartine.

SISTER MARIA LUISA, C.S.C., for her translation, "She Who Understands," from the Spanish of Alfonsina Storni.

SISTER MARY IMMACULATE, C.S.C., for her translation of "The Christ of the Fields" from the French of Francis Jammes, and for "God Spoke to Me" from the French of Paul Verlaine.

MARUSHA SMILYANICH, for her translation from the Italian of the selection from Dante's *Il Paradiso.*

ALEJANDRO A. STORNI, Larrea 1050, Buenos Aires, Argentina, for permission to translate into English the Spanish poem "La Que Comprende" by Alfonsina Storni, taken from *Antologia Poetica,* coleccion Austral, Espasa Calpe, Argentine, Buenos Aires, Argentina, copyright, 1942, by Espasa Calpe.

STUDENT CHRISTIAN MOVEMENT PRESS, for permission acknowledged under Harper and Row, Publishers, Inc.

THOUGHT, for "I Believe" by Daniel Berrigan, S.J., copyright, 1957, by *Thought.*

UNIVERSITY OF DETOIT PRESS, for "The Making of the Cross" by Brother Antoninus from *The Crooked Lines of God,* copyright, 1959, by the University of Detroit Press.

UNIVERSITY OF FLORIDA PRESS, for "Saint" by Kersti Merilaas from *An Anthology of Modern Estonian Poetry,* translated by W. K. Matthews, copyright, 1953, by University of Florida Press, reprinted by permission of Mrs. Naomi Matthews.

UNIVERSITY OF NOTRE DAME PRESS, for "In the Upper Room" by Charles L. O'Donnell, c.s.c. from *Collected Poems of Charles L. O'Donnell,* c.s.c. edited by Charles M. Carey, c.s.c., copyright, 1942, by the University of Notre Dame.

VANGUARD PRESS, for "Still Falls the Rain" by Edith Sitwell from *Collected Poems,* copyright, 1954, by Vanguard Press, reprinted by permission of Vanguard Press, and by permission also of the William Morris Agency and David Higham Associates, Ltd.

THE VIKING PRESS, INC., for the selection from *The Power and the Glory* by Graham Greene, copyright, 1946, by The Viking Press.

VOYAGES PRESS, for "The Wooden Christ" by Faustus Kirša, translated by Theodore Melnechuk, from *The Green Oak, Selected Lithuanian Poetry,* edited by Algirdas Landbergis and Clark Mills, copyright, 1962, by Voyages Press.

WASH'NGTON SQUARE PRESS, for "The Last Supper" by Oscar Williams from *A Pocket Book of Modern Verse,* edited by Oscar Williams, copyright, 1961, by the Washington Square Press, reprinted by permission of Oscar Williams.

ANN WOLFE, for permission acknowledged under Doubleday and Company, Inc.

YALE REVIEW, for "My Daughter on Good Friday" by Sheldon Tannenbaum, copyright, 1963, by *Yale Review.*

VARIOUS PUBLISHERS OF SCRIPTURAL TEXTS, for the selection from the Acts of the Apostles from *The Complete Bible, An American Translation,* translated from the Greek by J. M. Powis Smith, and Edgar J. Goodspeed, copyright, 1948, by University of Chicago Press; for Psalm 21, from *The Fides Translation of the Psalms,* copyright, 1955, by the Fides Publishers Association: for the selection from Isaiah, chapter 53, from *The Book of Isaiah* translated by the Reverend Edward J. Kissane, copyright, 1941, by Browne and Nolan, Ltd.; for the composite passage on the Passion according to Sts. Matthew, Mark, Luke, and John from *A Gospel Harmony,* edited by the Reverend John E. Steinmueller, copyright, 1942, by W. H. Sadlier; for the Epistles of St. Paul from *The Holy Bible* translated by Ronald Knox, copyright, 1950, by Sheed and Ward, Inc.; for the selection from the Apocalypse from *The New Testament* translated from the Latin Vulgate, edited by the Confraternity of Christian Doctrine, copyright, 1941, by St. Anthony Guild Press.

PREFACE

The story goes that a famous preacher once reduced his congregation to hysterical sobs by a sermon on the Passion. Dismayed by the success of his eloquence, he cried out: "Now, please, please don't be so upset. Remember this happened a very long time ago. Indeed, perhaps it never happened at all."

The story is, no doubt, apocryphal, but it illustrates a difficulty inherent in any faith which is based upon an historical revelation. The events recorded in the Gospels are past events which will never re-occur, but the faith which acknowledges their significance must, if it is to have any reality, be contemporary, renewed at each succeeding moment. We live in a world where, whether we are believers or unbelievers, devout, indifferent, or hostile, Christianity is a social fact, recognizable, not by faith alone but by the eye of flesh and blood. Churches are familiar objects in the landscape, we are accustomed to see people using them, and everybody has *some* notion, however inaccurate or distorted, of what those who call themselves Christians believe. Those of us who do go to church are apt to forget, when we recite the Creed, how little our conviction depends upon our personal faith, how much on the fact that for nearly two thousand years, in generation after generation, the laity have believed, prayed, partaken of the sacraments; priests have preached the Gospel and celebrated Mass, theologians have labored to define and clarify the meaning of the clauses we recite. That any of us today are Christians is in part due to cultural habit; for this we should thank God and our forebears, but we must not confuse habit with faith. If we do, we are in danger of fancying that had we been contemporaries of the historical Jesus, we would, of course, have instantly recognized Him as the Christ, the Word made flesh.

Another danger lies in the nature of human imagination which is indifferent to belief or disbelief and is only concerned with interesting possibilities. A poet, writing a poem about the Cross, may, as a man, be a devout Christian but, *qua* poet, it is all the same to him whether the Passion be an historical event or a myth. Again, as a poet, it is his business and duty to produce as beautiful and admirable a verbal object as possible, and this requires that he idealize reality. This is as it should be, provided neither he nor his readers confuse the poetic word with the Word of God. As an Austrian writer, Ferdinand Ebner, has said: "Both address themselves to the eternal in man; the poetic word speaks to the eternal ideal Thou in man, the Word of God to the eternal concrete Thou in him."

Of all the events narrated in the Gospels, the Crucifixion is the one which poetic idealization is most likely to falsify. Christmas and Easter, being in themselves happy and "beautiful" events, can be poeticized without much damage; Good Friday cannot. Those of us who live in civilized societies which have been strongly influenced by what, for want of a better word, is called humanitarianism, are more likely than previous generations to accept the idealization as reality. None of us has witnessed what even two hundred years ago was quite a common spectacle, a man being tortured to death in public, though we know only too well that were it to be announced in the press that tomorrow a criminal would be broken on the wheel in Times Square, a large crowd would gather, armed with field glasses and cameras.

It is important, though, that we make an effort to imagine what, had we stood on Golgotha, we should have seen.

It is not surprising that Christianity should sometimes be regarded as the darkest of superstitions, when it is considered that a thing of the lowest and most indecent horror should have been lifted, lit, and monstrously adored, and that not merely sensationally but by the vivid and philosophic assent of the great intellects of the Roman world. The worship in jungles and marshes, the intoxication of Oriental mysteries, had not hidden in incense and litany a more shocking idol. . . . The jewelled crosses hid one thing only—they hid the indecency. But original Crucifixion was precisely indecent. The images we still retain conceal—perhaps necessarily—the same thing; they preserve pain but they lack obscenity. But the dying agony of the God-Man exhibited both.

(Charles Williams: *The Descent of the Dove*)

Just as we were all in Adam, so were we all in those present in Jerusalem on that first Good Friday, and before reading this anthology and meditating upon the Passion of Our Lord as a redemptive act which for us now is a cause for rejoicing, we should do well, I think, to try to picture ourselves, in the light of what we know about ourselves, on that day when, as yet, there is no Easter, no Pentecost, no Church, no creed, and the word Christian has not been invented.

None of us, I fancy, would dare identify himself with the apostles, but, even if we did, we should find ourselves, not only in physical terror for our lives, but also in spiritual despair—the person who had come to such a dreadful end could not be what he had claimed and we had believed him to be. Even the three Marys and St. John, His mother and His dearest friends, standing beneath the Cross, stand there out of loyal affection to the Manhood, not in recognition of the Godhead. Few of us are devout enough to imagine ourselves as members of the Sanhedrin, or big wheels enough to imagine ourselves as Pilate, but if we are, which of us can honestly say that he would have acted any differently from the way they did? As for myself, the most optimistic image I can form is as follows: I am taking an afternoon stroll with a friend, the two of us engrossed in a philosophical argument. Our path takes us past Golgotha, and suddenly, there above us, is a familiar sight—three crosses and a crowd. With a superior sneer I remark to my friend: "Really, it's disgusting the way the mob enjoy such things. Why can't they kill criminals quickly and painlessly by giving them a draught of hemlock, as they did to Socrates?" Then I shut out the disagreeable picture from my mind, and we resume our fascinating discussion on the nature of the Beautiful.

If we make this preliminary effort we shall, I believe, be in a better position to appreciate Sister Mary Immaculate's excellent anthology. This is remarkable, both in its scholarship, its discriminating good taste, and the spirit of ecumenical charity which pervades it. The writers from whom she has taken selections are of many different temperaments and persuasions, Catholics, Protestants, humanists, skeptics, devout followers of the Cross, and rebels. Yet, after reading the whole book, one finds that what Sister Mary Immaculate says is true: "Unwittingly, these writers formed a pattern."

Every reader is going to find something in it which is new to him and, whatever his personal attitude to its theme may be, his heart will be stirred, his understanding clarified, and his desire aroused to reflect further upon the matter himself.

W. H. AUDEN

CONTENTS

II *IF I BE LIFTED UP*

III *THE MYSTERY AT THE CORE*

IV *IMAGE AND SYMBOL*

V THE DISCIPLE AND THE MASTER

VI *THE SIGN OF CONTRADICTION*

VII *THE GLORY TREE*

EPILOGUE

INTRODUCTION

In the Crucifixion of Jesus one finds the two basic themes of all literature, love and death. As both are here ordered to eternal life, this anthology follows events as they occurred from the Last Supper to the Resurrection.

The first division, which concerns the eucharistic feast, together with the agony and betrayal in Gethsemane, is titled "Forspent with Love and Shame." Following this, the redemption is contemplated under diverse aspects, appropriately placed in the schema according to the views taken by various writers. Some are interested in the fact of the Crucifixion, its historical significance, its paradoxical magnetism. These selections are grouped in the division "If I Be Lifted Up." Truths incompletely understood, usually ensuing from the union of the Victim's divine and human nature, are found in "The Mystery at the Core." Here, too, such antinomies as mercy and justice, ignominy and glory, anguish and peace, are juxtaposed or resolved. While figurative meanings abound throughout the anthology, the division "Image and Symbol" contains selections essentially dependent on these, or centered in the crucifix as a representation. In "The Disciple and the Master," the followers of and witnesses to the Crucified speak directly or through others. "The Sign of Contradiction" gives expression to doubts, questions, and rebellions, or brings into relief other facets of opposition to the cross. The final division, emphasizing the victory and splendor of the Resurrection, but always in relation to the cross, is titled "The Glory Tree."

Among writers of many ages, many cultures, many creeds, there was concurrence in the conviction that the death of Christ was a holocaust for all men, that its cause was the sin of all men, that its glory was the inheritance of all men who would accept its totality. As authors expressed what was most meaningful to them, however, complex attitudes developed. Unwittingly, these writers formed a pattern. Just as traditionally at the intersection of the cross there occurs a coincidence of opposites, the authors chosen produced from contrariety a unity of great beauty.

The attraction to the Cross being all but universal, I have endeavored to illustrate this world-wide appeal throughout the Christian centuries by selecting works from a number of languages, from many countries, and by writers of different faiths.

As a literary anthology, the work precludes expressly devotional and technically theological selections. Either of these provides a study for others to undertake.

Through the writers here assembled Christ may again so be lifted up as to draw at least some to himself.

Sister Mary Immaculate, c. s. c.
Saint Mary's College
Notre Dame, Indiana

I

FORSPENT WITH LOVE AND SHAME

> *Into the woods my Master came,*
> *Forspent with love and shame.*
> SIDNEY LANIER
> (1842-1881)

THE LASTING SUPPER
AND AFTER

And while they were at supper, Jesus took bread, and blessed and broke, and gave it to his disciples, and said, "Take and eat; this is my body." And taking a cup, he gave thanks and gave it to them saying, "All of you drink of this; for this is my blood of the new convenant, which is being shed for many unto the forgiveness of sins."

And while they were eating, he said, "Amen I say to you, one of you will betray me." And being very much saddened they began each to say, "Is it I, Lord?"

But he answered and said, "He who dips his hand with me in the dish, he will betray me. . . . It were better for that man if he had not been born."

And Judas who betrayed him answered and said, "Is it I, Rabbi?"

He said to him, "Thou hast said it."

Then Jesus came with them to a country place called Gethsemani, and he said to his disciples, "Sit down here, while I go over yonder and pray." And he took with him Peter and the two sons of Zebedee, and he began to be saddened and exceedingly troubled. Then he said to them, "My soul is sad, even unto death. Wait here and watch with me." And going forward a little, he fell on his face and prayed, saying, "Father, if it is possible let this cup pass away from me; yet not as I will, but as thou willest."

Then he came to the disciples and found them sleeping. And he said to Peter, "Could you not then watch one hour with me?

Watch and pray, that you may not enter into temptation. The spirit indeed is willing, but the flesh is weak."

And leaving them he went back again, and prayed a third time saying the same words over. Then he came to his disciples, and said to them, "Sleep on now, and take your rest! Behold, the hour is at hand, and the Son of Man will be betrayed into the hands of sinners. Rise, let us go. Behold, he who betrays me is at hand."

And while he was yet speaking, behold Judas, one of the Twelve, came and with him a crowd with swords and clubs, from the chief priests and elders of the people. Now his betrayer had given them a sign, saying, "Whomever I kiss, that is he; lay hold of him." And he went straight up to Jesus and said, "Hail Rabbi!" and kissed him.

And Jesus said to him, "Friend, for what purpose hast thou come?"

Then they came forward and set hands on Jesus and took him.

SAINT MATTHEW
26, *passim*

The Last Supper

They are gathered, astounded and disturbed,
round him who, like a sage resolved to his end,
takes himself away from those he belonged to,
and who alien past them flows.
The old loneliness comes over him
that reared him to the doing of his deep acts;
now again will he wander through the olive grove,
and those who love him will take flight before him.

He has summoned them to the last supper
and (as a shot scatters birds out of the sheaves)
he scatters their hands from among the loaves
with his word: they fly across to him;
they flutter anxious through the table's round
and try to find a way out. But he
is everywhere like a twilight-hour.

RAINER MARIA RILKE
(1875–1926)
Translated from the German by
M. D. Herter Norton

The Huckster

There were thirteen that ate together, drinking
strange wine, and biting on a perilous bread.
And one was speaking, and the rest were thinking
more of his eyes than of the things he said.
They were dark eyes, and in their deep was swaying

a mote of gold, that lit upon the word
subtly, as though the light in them were saying
    what, though unspoken, all, who listened, heard.
Most willingly they were caught in the gold's strand
    that bound their hearts only to set them free,
save one, who heard, but would not understand,
    afraid of blindness, if he dared to see.
But even so there was a ray of light
went out with him into the fatal night.

HUMBERT WOLFE
(1885–1940)

The Last Supper

I Apostles of the hidden sun
    Are come unto the room of breath
    Hung with the banging blinds of death,
    The body twelve, the spirit one,
    Far as the eye, in earth arrayed,
    The night shining, the supper laid.

II The wine shone on the table that evening of history
    Like an enormous ruby in the bauble and mystery.

In the glowing walls of the flickering decanter
There moved His face as at the world's center.

The hands of Judas showed up red and hurried
And light hit them so, like a cross carried.

The faces of the others were there and moving
In the crystal of the dome, swiftly hovering.

The saints, under a lens, shrunken to pigmies,
Gesticulated in birds or in colored enigmas.

Outside there was a storm, the sound of temblors,
The blood bubbled and sprang into the tumblers.

When the morning came like a wall of stone,
The day lay in the glass and the blood was gone.

OSCAR WILLIAMS
(1900–1964)

From Sherthursdaye and Venus Day

As a *paterfamilias* among his own on his own festal-night
empties out to the Genius of the place[1]
                              he in this place
empties himself
                              to the Lar of this place
of this household
                              in session, here
under the roof-beam at the bright hearth of
                              this Lar.

---

[1] Cf. the Roman domestic rites on the birthday of the head of the house which
was also the chief festival of the *genius* of the household. In making the
oblations the father offered in fact to his *own* Genius, to the "indwelling spirit
that gave the father of the family the power to prolong its existence." H. Stuart
Jones, *Companion to Roman History.*

Here, to the Genius of this *familia* of new-*gens* founders
inaugurally met.
Informed from before history proper:
> from the boundary-time.
They say that, once-upon-a-time, there was a duke without tree
the stirpless lord, a man of estate *sine genealogia*
> a rites-offerant
of an immutable *disciplina*.
Rex Pacis was his name
gentle, was his station.[2]
> Out from his dwelling place[3]
to the tithing of the spoil
> to take his war-dues.[4]
Our chrism'd Triptolemus
to quicken, to judge:
> the furrows
> the dead
from dear and grave Demeter come
> germ of all:
of the dear arts as well as bread.
To institute, to make stable
to offer oblations
> permanent
kindly, acceptable and valid:
> tillage fruit
> man's-norm

---

[2] Cf. Heb. vii.4 (A.V.), "consider how great this man was."
[3] Cf., e.g.,

> Alice Bradshaw is my name
> Simple is my station
> Rotherhithe my dwelling place
> And Christ my salvation.

[4] Gen. xiv.20.

then rational
             so food of angels.[5]
Munera
             of Liber, poured
             of Ceres, broken.
Not desert-rites, nor nomad-*liberi*.[6]
Levites! the new rite holds
                          is here
before your older rites begin.[7]
Here.
Where?
             Here when?
Here at the spoil-dump
at a war's term
where the high-flyer stalls
             after his concentric
and exact reconnaissance.[8]
Not every year is the salvage of so many inhabited places

---

[5] Cf. *Ecce panis angelorum* and "man is . . . Reasonable as an Aungell."
Triptolemus was sent by the Mother Goddess to initiate agriculture and settled
civilization and was also at Eleusis judge of the dead. He necessarily recalls
Melchesidec who appears as a priest of agriculture-rites in a pastoral setting
at the termination of a tribal war. If the significance of such types was brought
out by the author of Hebrews vii, the Roman liturgists from very early on had
given that significance special point and emphasis by relating it very immediately to the manual act of sacrifice, so that it continues still to be re-
asserted, every day, wherever a priest of the Roman rite asks that his offering
of the transubstantiated fruits of the earth shall be identified with and as
acceptable as "that which thy high priest Melchesidec offered up to thee."
(See the Roman Mass prayer *Supra quae propitio*, following close on the act
of consecration.)
[6] In the sense of young animals.
[7] Cf. Heb. vii.5-11 and the Maundy Thursday hymn, *Pange lingua*, verse 5.
Et antiquum documentum Novo cedat ritui: "And let an antique formula give
place to a new rite."
[8] Cf. the name of the hawk-headed god Horus which is said to mean "high-
flyer." I was thinking of the miscalled "eagles" that I saw in Egypt which seem
to stand still at a great height before they drop on something they have
sighted.

made legitimate loot. Not at every time are the cosmocrats
as prodigal or the bleached bodies so many, as now, in this
place.
In the wasted land
           at jackal-meet
at the division of the spoils
with his hands stretched out
                he continues.[9]

DAVID JONES
(1895–   )

The Dripping Blood Our Only Drink
From East Coker

    The dripping blood our only drink,
The bloody flesh our only food:
In spite of which we like to think
That we are sound, substantial flesh and blood—
Again, in spite of that, we call this Friday good.

T. S. ELIOT
(1888–1965)

The Burning Coal of the Godhead

The sacred Body of the Lord is a spiritualized body. The Fathers
call it the burning coal of the godhead. Glorified by the Spirit,

---

[9] See *Extensis manibus prosequitur*, the words of the rubric directing the
posture of the celebrant at the prayer in the mass beginning *Supra quae
propitio.*
NOTES BY DAVID JONES

the Lord's Body burns in the Spirit's glow. The Fathers compare
It also to a fragrant lily. The most holy Body of the Lord and
His divine-human Blood are filled with the fragrance of the
Holy Ghost. In particular, however, the Blood that flows in the
chalice is to the Fathers a sacramental symbol of the Holy Ghost.
If it is especially the sublime countenance of the Word that shines
in the sacred Host, it is the love of the Spirit that lives in the
eucharistic Wine, in the sacred Blood of the Lamb.

JULIUS TYCIAK
(1903–   )

He Bare Him Up

Lully, lulley, lully, lulley,
The fawcon hath born my make[1] away.

He bare hym up, he bare hym down,
He bare hym into an orchard browne.

In that orchard there was an halle
That was hangid with purpill and pall.

And in that hall there was a bede;[2]
Hit was hangid with gold so rede.

And yn that bed there lythe a knight,[3]
His wowndis bledyng day and nyght.

---

[1] Mate.   [2] Bed.   [3] The knight is Christ.

By that bedeside kneleth a may,[4]
And she wepeth both nyght and day.

And by that beddeside there stondith a ston,
'Corpus Christi' wretyn theron.

ANONYMOUS
(*c.* 1500)

The Holy Eucharist

Where hast thou gone, dear child,
Who looked to heaven and smiled,
From the gleaming
Earth, dreaming?

In woods and caverns thou art seen no more.
The air is harsh, the ground is dead and frore.

All her child-like flowers slain,
Nature will not smile again.
She is sick to death, and sear,
Pregnant with the fruitful year.
Yet, above the labouring root
Redden the ripe cheeks of fruit.
I will take thee, little one,
Nourished by the earth and sun,
Feed on thee in peace, and know
Nothing of thy mother's woe.

---

[4] Maid.

Wrinkled tree, like thee I stand
In the mighty orchard-land,
Wait as thou dost, to be fed
With the earth's unstinted bread.
Share thy strength with me, renew
My vanished sap and vigour too;
Humbly I would share thy meal,
Kneeling as the flowers kneel;
In thy leaves one mote of dust
Twinkling down the autumn gust.

Great thy power, O generous tree!
Courage, immortality,
Fill thee from thy groping root,
Fill me from thy basking fruit;
Circulation through one whole
Undivided perfect soul.
Mighty body, on thy flesh
I have fed, and live afresh:
Hallowed was that heavenly bread—
Why is all thy beauty dead?

Silence! Ah, the sweetness,
The colours that run through the vineyard with radiant fleetness!
The gladness that flashes through Nature's shadowed dwelling!
What is it that gleams and laughs where the grapes are swelling?

Exquisite grape, wine-ruddied,
Dark nature revives in thy flame, and is flooded
With light from thy locks as the sunbeams caress thee.
The shadow weaves
A face in the leaves,
And devoutly into the chalice I press thee.

And the angel who awoke the spring,
Whom sultry summer drove away
To the forest twilight-glimmering,
Is sparkling here in the purple spray.

The gentle flame, the river sound,
Light ether, spring's celestial friend,
The veil of flowers over the ground—
All fill this chalice at the end.

Lift the cup with reverent hands,
Stiff though they be with harvest frost,
Deep in the heart that understands
All blooms eternal, nothing lost.

Your withered creeds take root once more;
Your bread and wine are sacrificed;
Drink, heavenward gazing, and adore—
This is the blood of Jesus Christ.

ADAM OEHLENSCHLÄGER
(1779–1850)
*Translated from the Danish by
Robert S. Hillyer*

Barnfloor and Winepress

And he said, If the Lord do not help thee, whence
shall I help thee? Out of the barnfloor, or out of
the winepress?

II Kings vi.27

Thou that on sin's wages starvest,
Behold we have the joy in harvest:

For us was gather'd the first-fruits
For us was lifted from the roots,
Sheaved in cruel hands, bruised sore,
Scourged upon the threshing-floor;
Where the upper mill-stone roof'd His head,
At morn we found the heavenly Bread,
And on a thousand Altars laid,
Christ our Sacrifice is made.

Those whose dry plot for moisture gapes,
We shout with them that tread the grapes:
For us the Vine was fenced with thorn,
Five ways the precious branches torn;
Terrible fruit was on the tree
In the acre of Gethsemane;
For us by Calvary's distress
The wine was rackèd from the press;
Now in our altar-vessels stored
Is the sweet Vintage of our Lord.

In Joseph's garden they threw by
The riv'n Vine, leafless, lifeless, dry:
On Easter morn the Tree was forth,
In forty days reach'd Heaven from earth;
Soon the whole world is overspread;
Ye weary, come into the shade.

The field where He has planted us
Shall shake her fruit as Libanus,
When He has sheaved us in His sheaf,
When He has made us bear His leaf.—

We scarcely call that banquet food,
But even our Saviour's and our blood,
We are so grafted on His wood.

GERARD MANLEY HOPKINS
(1844–1889)

In the Upper Room

What did you hear last night, your head on His breast there?
It was Peter in the dark supper-room
Asking of John,
Who with Mary, His Mother, was just returned
From burying Him.

I heard His blood moving like an unborn child,
And His Heart crying.
I heard Him talking with His Father
And the Dove.
I heard an undertone as of the sea swinging, and a whispering at
   its centre.
I listened, and all the sound
Was a murmuring of names.
I heard my own name beating in His Blood,
And yours, Peter,
And all of you.
And I heard Judas,
And the names of all that have been
Or shall be to the last day.

And it was His Blood was calling out these names,
And they possessed His Blood.

Did you hear my name?
Asked a woman who was sitting at His Mother's feet.
I heard your name, Mary of Magdala, and it was like a storm at
    sea
And the waves racing.
I heard Peter's name,
And the sea broke, I thought, and ran over the world.
You heard then the name of Mary, His Mother, Peter said quietly,
    as he wept there kneeling.
I did, and it was like the singing of winds and they moving over
    an ocean of stars, and every star like a hushed child sleeping.

Again Peter—
What of Iscariot?
I heard the tide come in, and I felt the tide go out,
And I saw a dead man washed upon the shore.

And then John fell to weeping, and no one there could comfort him
    but only Mary, the Mother of Jesus, and he could tell them
No other word.

CHARLES L. O'DONNELL, C.S.C.
(1884–1934)

Our Lord's Mental Sufferings

Our Lord said, when His agony was commencing, "My soul is
sorrowful unto death"; now you may ask, my Brethren, whether
He had not certain consolations peculiar to Himself, impossible

in any other, which diminished or impeded the distress of His soul, and caused Him to feel, not more, but less than an ordinary man. For instance, He had a sense of innocence which no other sufferer could have; even His persecutors, even the false Apostle who betrayed Him, the judge who sentenced Him, and the soldiers who conducted the execution, testified His innocence. "I have condemned the innocent blood," said Judas; "I am clear from the blood of this just Person," said Pilate; "Truly this was a just Man," cried the centurion. And if even they, sinners, bore witness to His sinlessness, how much more did His own soul! And we know well that even in our own case, sinners as we are, on the consciousness of innocence or of guilt mainly turns our power to enduring opposition and calumny; how much more, you will say, in the case of our Lord, did the sense of inward sanctity compensate for the suffering and annihilate the shame! Again, you may say that He knew that His sufferings would be short, and that their issue would be joyful, whereas uncertainty of the future is the keenest element of human distress; but He could not have anxiety, for He was not in suspense; nor despondency or despair, for He never was deserted. And in confirmation you may refer to St. Paul, who expressly tells us that, "for the joy set before Him," our Lord "despised the shame." And certainly there is a marvelous calm and self-possession in all He does: consider His warning to the Apostles, "Watch and pray, lest ye enter into temptation; the spirit indeed is willing, but the flesh is weak"; or His words to Judas, "Friend, wherefor art thou come?" and, "Judas, betrayest thou the Son of Man with a kiss?" or to Peter, "All that take the sword shall perish with the sword"; or to the man who struck Him, "If I have spoken evil, bear witness of the evil; but if well, why smitest thou Me?" or to His Mother, "Woman, behold thy Son."

All this is true and much to be insisted on; but it quite agrees with, or rather illustrates, what I have been observing. My

Brethren, you have only said (to use a human phrase) that He was always Himself. His mind was its own center, and was never in the slightest degree thrown off its heavenly and most perfect balance. What He suffered, He suffered because He put Himself under suffering, and that deliberately and calmly. . . . His composure is but the proof how entirely He governed His own mind. He drew back, at the proper moment, the bolts and fastenings, and opened the gates, and the floods fell right upon His soul in all their fullness. That is what St. Mark tells us of Him; and he is said to have written his Gospels from the very mouth of St. Peter, who was one of three witnesses present at the time. "They came," he says, "to the place which is called Gethsemani; and He saith to His disciples, Sit you here while I pray. And He taketh with Him Peter and James and John, and He *began to be* frightened and to be very heavy." You see how deliberately He acts; He comes to a certain spot; and then, giving the word of command, and withdrawing the support of the Godhead from His soul, distress, terror, and dejection at once rush in upon it. Thus He walks forth into a mental agony with as definite an action as if it were some bodily torture, the fire or the wheel.

This being the case, you will see at once, my Brethren, that it is nothing to the purpose to say that He would be supported under His trial by the consciousness of innocence and the anticipation of triumph; for His trial consisted in the withdrawal, as of other causes of consolation, so of that very consciousness and anticipation. The same act of the will which admitted the influence upon His soul of any distress at all, admitted all distresses at once. It was not the contest between antagonist impulses and views, coming from without, but the operation of an inward resolution. As men of self-command can turn from one thought to another at their will, so much more did He deliberately deny Himself the comfort, and satiate Himself with the woe. In that moment His soul thought not of the future, He thought only of the present burden which was upon Him, and which He had come upon earth to sustain.

And now, my Brethren, what was it He had to bear, when He thus opened upon His soul the torrent of this predestinated pain? Alas! He had to bear what is well known to us, what is familiar to us, but what to Him was woe unutterable. He had to bear that which is so easy a thing to us, so natural, so welcome, that we cannot conceive of it as a great endurance, but which to Him had the scent and the poison of death—He had, my dear Brethren, to bear the weight of sin; He had to bear your sins; He had to bear the sins of the whole world.

JOHN HENRY CARDINAL NEWMAN
(1801–1890)

Ballad of the Trees and the Master

Into the woods my Master went,
Clean forspent, forspent.
Into the woods my Master came,
Forspent with love and shame.
But the olives they were not blind to Him,
The little gray leaves were kind to Him:
The thorn-tree had a mind to Him
When into the woods He came.

Out of the woods my Master went,
And he was well content.

Out of the woods my Master came,
Content with death and shame.
When Death and Shame would woo Him last,
From under the trees they drew Him last:
'Twas on a tree they slew Him—last
When out of the woods He came.

SIDNEY LANIER
(1842–1881)

Sin's Heavy Load

O Lord, my sin doth overcharge Thy breast.
   Thy poise[1] thereof doth force Thy knees to bow;
Yea, flat Thou fallest with my faults oppressed,
   And bloody sweat runs trickling from Thy brow:
But had they not to earth thus pressèd Thee,
Much more they would in hell have pestred[2] me.

This globe of earth doth Thy one finger prop,
   The world Thou dost within Thy hand embrace;
Yet all this weight, of sweat drew not a drop
   Nor made Thee bow, much less fall on Thy face;
But now Thou hast a load so heavy found,
That makes Thee bow, yea, flat fall to the ground.

O Sin! how huge and heavy is thy weight,
   That weighest more than all the world beside;
Of which when Christ had taken in his freight,
   The poise[1] thereof His flesh could not abide.

---

[1] Weight.   [2] Tortured.

Alas! if God Himself sink under sin,
What will become of man that dies therein?

First flat Thou fellest where earth did Thee receive,
    In closet[3] pure of Mary's virgin breast;
And now Thou fallst, of earth to take Thy leave,
    Thou kissest it as cause of Thy unrest:
O loving Lord! that so dost love Thy foe
As thus to kiss the ground where he doth go!

Thou, minded in Thy heaven our earth to wear,
    Dost prostrate now Thy heaven our earth to bliss;
As God to earth Thou often wert severe,
    As man Thou sealst a peace with bleeding kiss:
For as of souls Thou common father art,
So is she mother of man's other part.

She shortly was to drink Thy dearest blood,
    And yield Thy soul away to Satan's cave;
She shortly was Thy cors[4] in tomb to shroud,
    And with them all Thy Deity to have;
Now then in one Thou jointly yieldest all,
That severally to earth should shortly fall.

O prostrate Christ! erect my crooked mind;
    Lord, let Thy fall my flight from earth obtain:
Or if I still in earth must needs be shrined,
    Then, Lord! on earth come fall yet once again;

---

[3] Enclosure.   [4] Body.

And either yield me in earth to lie,
Or else with Thee to take me to the sky.

BLESSED ROBERT SOUTHWELL
(1561?–1595)

ᘛ᙮ᘚ᙮ᘛ᙮ᘚ᙮ᘛ᙮ᘚ᙮ᘛ᙮ᘚ᙮ᘛ᙮ᘚ

Night in the Lonely Garden

In His passion, Jesus undergoes the sufferings that men cause Him; but in His agony, He endures the anguish He gives Himself: *He troubled himself*. It is the torture of a hand that is not human but omnipotent because one must be omnipotent to bear it.

Jesus seeks some comfort, at least from His three dearest friends, and they are asleep; He entreats them to watch a little with Him, and they desert Him with complete heedlessness, possessed of so little compassion that it did not even prevent them from sleeping a while. And thus Jesus was abandoned alone to the wrath of God.

Jesus is alone on earth, not only alone to experience and partake of His sufferings but even to know it: Heaven and He alone share in this knowledge.

Jesus is in a garden, not in a garden of delight like the first Adam, wherein he caused the ruin of himself and the whole human race, but in a garden of torments wherein He delivered Himself and the whole human race.

He suffers this pain and desertion in the horror of the night.

I think that Jesus never complained but this once; but at that time He complains as if no longer able to curb His excessive grief: *My soul is sorrowful even unto death*.

Jesus seeks the companionship and comfort of men. That is unique in His whole life, I think. But He receives none, because His disciples are sleeping.

Jesus will be in agony until the end of the world; we must not sleep during that time.

In the midst of this universal abandonment, and that by His friends chosen to watch with Him, Jesus, finding them asleep, grows angry because of the danger to which they expose, not Him, but themselves; and He admonishes them of their own salvation and of their own interest with a heartfelt tenderness for them in the midst of their ingratitude, and warns them that the spirit is willing but the flesh weak.

Finding them still sleeping, not restrained therefrom by any consideration for Him or for themselves, Jesus has the kindness not to awaken them but leaves them to their rest.

Jesus prays . . . as to His Father's will, and fears death; but, having known it, He goes forward to offer Himself to it: *Let us go. He went forth.* (Joannes).

Jesus entreated men, but His prayer was not heard by them.

While His disciples slept, Jesus effected their salvation. He did it for each of them just as they slept, both in their nothingness before their birth, as well as in their sins after their birth.

He prays but once that the chalice pass away and nevertheless submissively, and twice that it may come if it must. . . .

In Judas, Jesus does not behold his enmity, but the order of God Whom He loves, and He confesses it since He calls him friend.

Jesus tears Himself away from His disciples to enter upon His agony; we must tear ourselves away from our closest and dearest ones to imitate Him.

When Jesus is in the midst of His agony and His greatest pains, let us pray the longer.

We implore the mercy of God, not that He may leave us in peace
in the midst of our vices, but that He deliver us from them.

Blaise Pascal
(1623–1662)

Gethsemane

In the garden Jesus knelt, his eyes closed
And his face to the earth. The wind drew forth his sighs.
A spring that mirrored the faint disk of the moon
Murmured its sorrow. It was the hour when the weeping angel
From the throne of God came bearing the cup of sorrow.

Before the Saviour stood the Cross.
Torn, stretched upon it, he saw his own body,
His sinews like ropes beneath the skin.
He saw the nails come through, the crown
With its single thorns bleeding.
In halted voice, the thunder rumbled its anger.
Then down the beam of the cross he heard drops falling,
And a cry lost in torture.
Then Jesus sighed, and crimson sweat rained down.

In darkness night grew deeper.
A dead sun swam in the gray sea.
Scarce to be seen was his violent shuddering,
The writhing head that tossed in agony to and fro.

At the foot of the Cross three figures lay.
He saw them lying, gray as shapes of fog;

He heard the rapid flight of their breath,
The rustle their trembling made in the folds of their garments.
What love burned like his?
Deeply discerning their hearts, he knew them.
The blood in Jesus' veins stood still,
Then in heavier sweat gushed out.

In the spot where the sun disappeared was black smoke;
In it the Cross vanished, and the sighs.
More dread than raging thunder,
Through the starless paths of air, silence fell.
Wide and far across the earth no life breathed.
Round about it a crater burned, broad and empty,
And a hollow voice above it cried,
"God, my God, why hast thou forsaken me?"
Then Jesus was seized by death throes,
And with broken voice he wept,
"If it can be, let not this hour come!"

A streak of lightning pierced the night.
In its light moved the Cross,
Splendid with the signs of the Victim.
Grasping in fear toward the bleeding beam,
Reached millions of hands, hands large and small,
Hands from the utmost realms. Like sparks hovering
About the crown moved millions yet unborn,
And the prayers of the dead rose from the graves
Like soft mists from the ground.
Then Jesus stood up in the fulness of love and cried,
"Father, Father! Thy will, not mine, be done."

Silently the moon floated in the blue.
The stem of a lily stood before Jesus

In the dew-drenched green.
From the chalice of the lily an angel stepped forth
Comforting him.

ANNETTE VON DRÖSTE-HÜLSHOFF
(1797–1848)
Translated from the German by
Frida Grosser

Mary at Canne

A chaste moon rises between Eben and Canne.
It's the hour when Mary must be gone

Across the hills and the gentle sweep
Of the dusky dale in its white sleep.

The poplars tremble; the brook, among
Flowers and sedge, sings an age-old song.

She appears on top of the darkened wold,
By her own radiance aureoled:

In front of the marl pit a silver flame,
White vision in a dream's dark frame.

Her feet touch the valley with tender love,
As the dusk is tapped by the wings of a dove.

She holds in check with violet wreaths
Her wealth of hair blown by the breeze.

Her face lily-still. On the pure scale
Of her little hand sings a nightingale.

A delicate doe on a silken lead
Gambols ahead on the flowery mead.

At the fork she kisses the wounds of her son,
Who died for the sins of everyone.

The nail holes turn into roses, bright
With purple heat in the moon's cool light.

She shakes the trees, and a red rain
Of apple blossoms drops on the plain.

Straight at me she comes—but not to me—
And hovers past me smilingly

To where a little sleepy-eyes
Dreams on the slope and finds paradise.

She lays her hands on the little boy.
He rises and sings in radiant joy.

She offers to the purity of that face
The cradle of her arms with bending grace.

And carries the child across the spray
Of brook and fall, and speeds away.

"O Virgin Mother of charity,
Look for the child in my poverty,"

I said and ran after her. Once again
I heard the nightingale's refrain.

In the black mouth of the quarry's pit
A silvery light: In the midst of it

A guilty man who betrayed her son.
The moon comes up between Eben and Canne.

Jan Engelman
(1900–   )
Translated from the Dutch by
Adriaan J. Barnouw

II ❧

IF I BE LIFTED UP

And I, if I be lifted up from the earth,
will draw all things to myself.
SAINT JOHN 12:32

O crux, ave, spes unica!
VENANTIUS FORTUNATUS (530?-610?)

SEVEN UNDYING WORDS

And they came to the place called the Skull. They crucified him there, and the robbers, one on his right hand and the other on his left. And Jesus said, "Father, forgive them, for they do not know what they are doing."

Now one of those robbers who were hanged was abusing him, saying, "If thou art the Christ, save thyself and us!" But the other in answer rebuked him and said, "Dost thou not even fear God, seeing that thou art under the same sentence? And we indeed justly, for we are receiving what our deeds deserved; but this man has done nothing wrong." And he said to Jesus, "Lord, remember me when thou comest into thy kingdom." And Jesus said to him, "Amen I say to thee, this day thou shalt be with me in paradise."

Now there was standing by the cross of Jesus his mother and his mother's sister, Mary of Cleophas, and Mary Magdalene. When Jesus, therefore, saw his mother and the disciple standing by, whom he loved, he said to his mother, "Woman, behold thy son." Then he said to the disciple, "Behold thy mother." And from that hour the disciple took her into his home.

And at the ninth hour Jesus cried out with a loud voice, saying, "Eloi, Eloi, lama sabacthani?" which, translated, is "My God, my God, why hast thou forsaken me?" And some of the bystanders on hearing this said, "Behold, he is calling Elias."

After this, Jesus knowing that all things were now accomplished, that the Scripture might be fulfilled, said, "I thirst." And immediately one of them ran and, taking a sponge, soaked it in common wine, put it on a reed and offered it to him to drink. But the rest said, *"Wait, let us see whether Elias is coming to save him."*

Therefore, *when Jesus had taken the wine, he said, "It is con-* Finished. *summated!"*

And behold, the curtain of the temple was torn in two from top to bottom. And Jesus cried out with a loud voice and said, "Father, into thy hands I commend my spirit," and yielded up his spirit as he said it.

Now when the centurion, who stood facing him, saw how he had thus cried out and expired, he said, "Truly this man was the Son of God."[1]

---

[1] This selection is a composite of Matt. xxvii, Mark xv, Luke xxiii, John xix, *passim.*

The Meaning of the Cross

The Cross has always been a symbol of conflict and a principle of selection among men. The Faith tells us that it is by the willed attraction or repulsion exercised upon souls by the Cross that the sorting of the good seed from the bad, the separation of the chosen elements from the unutilizable ones, is accomplished at the heart of mankind. Wherever the Cross appears, unrest and antagonisms are inevitable. But there is no reason why these conflicts should be needlessly exacerbated by preaching the doctrine of Christ crucified in a discordant or provocative manner. Far too often the Cross is presented for our adoration, not so much as a sublime end to be attained by our transcending ourselves, but as a symbol of sadness, of limitation and repression.

This way of preaching the Passion is, in many cases, merely the result of the inept use of pious vocabulary in which the most solemn words (sacrifice, immolation, expiation), devoided of their meaning by routine, are used, quite unconsciously, in a light and frivolous way. They become formulas to be juggled with. But this manner of speech ends by conveying the impression that the Kingdom of God can only be established in mourning, and by thwarting and going against the current of man's aspirations and energies. By words that are, in themselves, faithful to their meaning, a picture is revealed than which nothing could really be less Christian. . . .

In its highest and most general sense, the doctrine of the Cross is that to which all men adhere who believe that the vast movement and agitation of human life opens on to a road which leads somewhere, and that that road *climbs upward*. Life has a term: therefore it imposes a particular direction, orientated, in fact, towards the highest possible spiritualization by means of the greatest possible effort. To admit that group of fundamental principles is already to range oneself among the disciples—distant, perhaps, and implicit, but nevertheless real—of Christ Crucified. Once that first choice has been made, the first distinction has been drawn between the brave who will succeed and the pleasure-seekers who will fail, between the elect and the condemned.

This rather vague attitude is clarified and carried further by Christianity. Above all, by revealing an original fall, Christianity provides our intelligence with a reason for the disconcerting excess of sin and suffering at certain points. Next, in order to win our love and secure our faith, it unveils to our eyes and hearts the moving and unfathomable reality of the historical Christ in whom the exemplary life of an individual man conceals this mysterious drama: the Master of the world, leading, like an element of the world, not only an elemental life, but (in addition to this and because of it) leading the total life of the universe, which He has shouldered and assimilated by experiencing it Himself. And finally, by the crucifixion and death of this adored Being, Christianity signifies to our thirst for happiness that the term of creation is not to be sought in the temporal zones of our visible world, but that the effort required of our fidelity must be consummated *beyond a total metamorphosis* of ourselves and of everything surrounding us.

Thus the perspectives of renunciation implied in the exercise of life itself are gradually expanded. Ultimately we find ourselves thoroughly uprooted, as the Gospel desires, from everything tangible on earth. But the process of uprooting ourselves has happened little by little and according to a rhythm which has neither alarmed nor wounded the respect we owe to the admirable beauties of the human effort.

It is perfectly true that the Cross means going beyond the frontiers of the sensible world and even, in a sense, breaking with it. The final stages of the ascent to which it calls us compel us to cross a threshold, a critical point, where we lose touch with the zone of the realities of the senses. That final "excess," glimpsed and accepted from the first steps, inevitably puts everything we do in a special light and gives it a particular significance. That is exactly where the folly of Christianity lies in the eyes of the "wise" who are not prepared to stake the good which they now hold in their hands on a total "Beyond." But that agonizing flight from the experimental zones—which is what the Cross means—is only (as should be strongly emphasized) the sublime aspect of a law common to *all* life. Towards the summit, wrapped in mist to our human eyes and to which the Cross invites us, we rise by a path which is the way of universal progress. The royal road of the Cross is no more nor less than the road of human endeavour supernaturally righted and prolonged. Once we have fully grasped the meaning of the Cross, we are no longer in danger of finding life sad and ugly. We shall simply have become more attentive to its incomprehensible gravity.

To sum up, Jesus on the Cross is both the symbol and the reality of the immense labour of the centuries which has, little by little, raised up the created spirit and brought it back to the depths of the divine context. He represents (and in a true sense, He is) creation, as, sustained by God, it re-ascends the slopes of being, sometimes clinging to things for support, sometimes tearing itself from them in order to transcend them, and always compensating, by physical suffering, for the setbacks caused by its moral downfalls.

The Cross is therefore not inhuman but superhuman. We can now understand that from the very first, from the very origins of mankind as we know it, the Cross was placed on the crest of the road which leads to the highest peaks of creation. But, in the growing light of revelation, its arms, which at first were bare, show themselves to have put on Christ: *Crux inuncta*. At first sight the bleeding body may seem mournful to us. Is it not from the night that it shines forth? But if we go nearer we shall recognize the flaming Seraphim of Alvernia whose passion and compassion are *incendium mentis*. The Christian is not asked to swoon in the shadow, but to climb in the light.

PIERRE TEILHARD DE CHARDIN
(1881–1955)

The Crucifixion

At the cry of the first bird
They began to crucify Thee, O cheek like a swan;
It were not right ever to cease lamenting—
It was like the parting of day from night.

Ah! though sore the suffering
Put upon the body of Mary's Son—
Sorer to Him was the grief
That was upon her for His sake.

ANONYMOUS (12TH CENTURY), IRISH
Translated from the Gaelic by
Kuno Meyer

A Dream of the Rood

Lo! I will tell   the dearest of dreams
That I dreamed in the midnight   when mortal men
Were sunk in slumber.   Me-seemed I saw

A wondrous Tree   towering in air,
Most shining of crosses   compassed with light.
Brightly that beacon   was gilded with gold;
Jewels adorned it   fair at the foot,
Five on the shoulder-beam,   blazing in splendour.
Through all creation   the angels of God
Beheld it shining—   no cross of shame!
Holy spirits   gazed on its gleaming,
Men upon earth   and all this great creation.
   Wondrous that Tree,   that Token of triumph,
And I a transgressor   soiled with my sins!
I gazed on the Rood   arrayed in glory,
Shining in beauty   and gilded with gold,
The Cross of the Saviour   beset with gems.
But through the gold-work   outgleamed a token
Of the ancient evil   of sinful men
Where the Rood on its right side   once sweat blood.
Saddened and rueful,   smitten with terror
At the wondrous Vision,   I saw the Cross
Swiftly varying   vesture and hue,
Now wet and stained   with the Blood outwelling,
Now fairly jewelled   with gold and gems.
   Then, as I lay there,   long I gazed
In rue and sadness   on my Saviour's Tree,
Till I heard in dream   how the Cross addressed me,
Of all woods worthiest,   speaking these words:
   "Long years ago   (well yet I remember)
They hewed me down   on the edge of the holt,
Severed my trunk;   strong foemen took me,
For a spectacle wrought me,   a gallows for rogues.
High on their shoulders   they bore me to hilltop,
Fastened me firmly,   an army of foes!

"Then I saw the King   of all mankind
In brave mood hasting   to mount upon me.
Refuse I dared not,   nor bow nor break
Though I felt earth's confines   shudder in fear;
All foes I might fell,   yet still I stood fast.
"Then the young Warrior,   God, the All-Wielder,
Put off his raiment,   steadfast and strong;
With lordly mood   in the sight of many
He mounted the Cross   to redeem mankind.
When the Hero clasped me   I trembled in terror,
But I dared not bow me   nor bend to earth;
I must needs stand fast.   Upraised as the Rood
I held the High King,   the Lord of heaven.
I dared not bow!   With black nails driven
Those sinners pierced me;   the prints are clear,
The open wounds.   I dared injure none.
They mocked us both.   I was wet with blood
From the Hero's side   when He sent forth His spirit.
"Many a bale   I bore on that hill-side
Seeing the Lord   in agony outstretched.
Black darkness covered   with clouds God's Body,
That radiant splendour.   Shadow went forth
Wan under heaven;   all creation wept
Bewailing the King's death.   Christ was on the Cross.
"Then many came quickly,   faring from far,
Hurrying to the Prince.   I beheld it all.
Sorely smitten with sorrow   in meekness I bowed
To the hands of men.   From His heavy and bitter pain
They lifted Almighty God.   Those warriors left me
Standing bespattered with blood;   I was wounded with spears.
Limb-weary they laid Him down;   they stood at His head,
Looked on the Lord of heaven   as He lay there at rest
From His bitter ordeal all forspent.   In sight of His slayers

They made Him a sepulchre   carved from the shining stone;
Therein laid the Lord of triumph.   At evening tide
Sadly they sang their dirges   and wearily turned away
From their lordly Prince;   there He lay all still and alone.
     "There at our station   a long time we stood
Sorrowfully weeping   after the wailing of men
Had died away.   The corpse grew cold,
The fair life-dwelling.   Down to earth
Men hacked and felled us,   a grievous fate!
They dug a pit   and buried us deep.
But there God's friends   and followers found me
And graced me with treasure   of silver and gold.
     "Now may you learn,   O man beloved,
The bitter sorrows   that I have borne,
The work of caitiffs.   But the time is come
That men upon earth   and through all creation
Show me honour   and bow to this sign.
On me a while   God's Son once suffered;
Now I tower under heaven   in glory attired
With healing for all   that hold me in awe.
Of old I was once   the most woeful of tortures,
Most hateful to all men,   till I opened for them
The true Way of life.   Lo! the Lord of glory,
The Warden of heaven,   above all wood
Has glorified me   as Almighty God
Has honoured His mother,   even Mary herself,
Over all womankind   in the eyes of men.
     "Now I give you bidding,   O man beloved,
Reveal this Vision   to the sons of men,
And clearly tell   of the Tree of glory
Whereon God suffered   for man's many sins
And the evil that Adam   once wrought of old.
     "Death He suffered,   but our Saviour rose

By virtue of His great might   as a help to men.
He ascended to heaven.   But hither again
He shall come unto earth   to seek mankind,
The Lord Himself   on the Day of Doom,
Almighty God   with His angel hosts.
And then will He judge,   Who has power of judgment,
To each man according   as here on earth
In this fleeting life   he shall win reward.
    "Nor there may any   be free from fear
Hearing the words   which the Wielder shall utter.
He shall ask before many: Where is the man
Who would taste bitter death   as He did on the Tree?
And all shall be fearful   and few shall know
What to say unto Christ.   But none at His Coming
Shall need to fear   if he bears in his breast
This best of symbols;   and every soul
From the ways of earth   through the Cross shall come
To heavenly glory,   who would dwell with God."
    Then with ardent spirit   and earnest zeal,
Companionless, lonely,   I prayed to the Cross.
My soul was fain of death.   I had endured
Many an hour of longing.   It is my life's hope
That I may turn   to this Token of triumph,
I above all men,   and revere it well.
    This is my heart's desire,   and all my hope
Waits on the Cross.   In this world now
I have few powerful friends;   they have fared hence
Away from these earthly gauds   seeking the King of glory,
Dwelling now with the High Father   in heaven above,
Abiding in rapture.   Each day I dream
Of the hour when the Cross of my Lord,   whereof here on earth
I once had vision,   from this fleeting life may fetch me
And bring me where is great gladness   and heavenly bliss,

Where the people of God   are planted and stablished for ever
In joy everlasting.   There may it lodge me
Where I may abide in glory   knowing bliss with the saints.
   May the Lord befriend me   who on earth of old
Once suffered on the Cross   for the sins of men.
He redeemed us, endowed us with life   and a heavenly home.
Therein was hope renewed   with blessing and bliss
For those who endured the burning.   In that great deed
God's Son was triumphant,   possessing power and strength!
Almighty, Sole-Ruling   He came to the kingdom of God
Bringing a host of souls   to angelic bliss,
To join the saints   who abode in the splendour of glory,
When the Lord, Almighty God,   came again to His throne.

ANONYMOUS
(8th century)
Translated from the Old English by
Charles W. Kennedy

Sunset on Calvary

Now goeth the sun under the wood,—
I rue, Marie, thy fair rode.[1]
Now goeth the sun under the tree,—
I rue, Marie, thy son and thee.

ANONYMOUS
(13th century)

---

[1] Color; hue; here probably face or countenance.

Whether Christ Ought To Have Suffered on the Cross

It was most fitting that Christ should suffer the death of the cross, first of all, as an example of virtue. For Augustine thus writes (QQ. lxxxiii, qu. 25): "God's Wisdom became man to give us an example in righteousness of living. But it is part of righteous living not to stand in fear of things which ought not to be feared. Now there are some men who, although they do not fear death in itself, are yet troubled over the manner of their death. In order, then, that no kind of death should trouble an upright man, the cross of this Man had to be set before him, because, among all kinds of death, none was more execrable, more fear-inspiring, than this."

Secondly, because this kind of death was especially suitable in order to atone for the sin of our first parent, which was the plucking of the apple from the forbidden tree against God's command. And so, to atone for that sin, it was fitting that Christ should suffer by being fastened to a tree, as if restoring what Adam had purloined; according to Ps. lxviii.5: "Then did I pay that which I took not away." Hence Augustine says in a sermon on the Passion:[1] "Adam despised the command, plucking the apple from the tree: but all that Adam lost, Christ found upon the cross."

The third reason is because, as Chrysostom says in a sermon on the Passion (De Cruce et Latrone i, ii): "He suffered upon a high rood and not under a roof, in order that the nature of the air might be purified: and the earth felt a like benefit, for it was cleansed by the flowing of the blood from His side." And on John iii.14: "The Son of man must be lifted up," Theophylact says: "When you

---

[1] Cf. *Serm.* ci, *De Tempore.*

hear that He was lifted up, understand His hanging on high, that He might sanctify the air who had sanctified the earth by walking upon it."

The fourth reason is, because, by dying on it, He prepares for us an ascent into heaven, as Chrysostom[2] says. Hence it is that He says (John xii.32): "If I be lifted up from the earth, I will draw all things to Myself."

The fifth reason is because it is befitting the universal salvation of the entire world. Hence Gregory of Nyssa observes (In Christ. Ressurr., Orat. i) that "the shape of the cross extending out into four extremes from their central point of contact denotes the power and the providence diffused everywhere of Him who hung upon it." Chrysostom[3] also says that upon the cross "He dies with outstretched hands in order to draw with one hand the people of old, and with the other those who spring from the Gentiles."

The sixth reason is because of the various virtues denoted by this class of death. Hence Augustine in his book on the grace of the Old and New Testament (Ep. cxl) says: "Not without purpose did He choose this class of death, that He might be a teacher of that breadth, and height, and length, and depth, of which the Apostle speaks (Eph. iii.18): For breadth is in the beam, which is fixed transversely above; this appertains to good works, since the hands are stretched out upon it. Length is the tree's extent from the beam to the ground; and there it is planted—that is, it stands and abides—which is the note of longanimity. Height is in that portion of the tree which remains over from the transverse beam upwards to the top, and this is at the head of the Crucified, because He is the supreme desire of souls of good hope. But that part of the tree which is hidden from view to hold it fixed, and from which the entire rood springs, denotes the depth of gratuitous grace." And, as Augustine says (Tract. cxix, in Joan.): "The tree upon

---

[2] Athanasius, *vide A.* iii, *ad* 2.   [3] Athanasius, *ibid.*

which were fixed the members of Him dying was even the chair of
the Master teaching."

The seventh reason is because this kind of death responds to
very many figures. For, as Augustine says in a sermon on the Passion (*loc. cit.*), an ark of wood preserved the human race from
the waters of the Deluge; at the exodus of God's people from
Egypt, Moses with a rod divided the sea, overthrew Pharaoh and
saved the people of God; the same Moses dipped his rod into the
water, changing it from bitter to sweet; at the touch of a wooden
rod a salutary spring gushed forth from a spiritual rock; likewise,
in order to overcome Amalec, Moses stretched forth his arms with
rod in hand; lastly, God's law is entrusted to the wooden Ark of
the Covenant; all of which are like steps by which we mount to the
wood of the cross.

SAINT THOMAS AQUINAS
(1225–1274)

Rose
From The Christ of Velázquez, Part One, XIII

Thy body, like the wild rose of the bramble
with five white petals, is the perfect flower
of creation; thy full heart, where Thou dost
distil the essence of the cream of life,
is its blood-stained chalice. Sorrow filled it
to the very brim, vessel of the fathomless
anguish that the mortal breast cannot hold;
from Thee, divine Master, we learn of sorrow,
the sorrows from whence hope springs. Thou didst
taste
of the sorrow that kills man; suffering thus

for us Thou didst kill fear. And by thy pain
that did make God Man, Brother, we love Thee
and our Father is common, ours and Thine,
by thy sorrow, divine Master of sorrows,
since thy divinity it is that teaches!

Thou art like the wild white rose of the bramble
with its five petals—a bramble thy cross,
thy bed of thorns—thy body is as white

Ex. III, 2   as the rose of the bush that burned with fire
on the mount of God and was not consumed,
a taper of flame in the midst of briars
is the white fire of thine eternal love.
And in Thee, flame of love, flowering bramble,
as to Moses, thy Father speaks to us,

Ex. III, 14   murmuring softly: "I am that I am!"
But the calyx of the rose is thy mouth,
which is the comb of honey where the souls,
bees, go straight to sip, thy mouth filled with
    flowers
of the field, parables that find a way
to our hearts. It has closed in the cold night,
and thy two lips are like another wound;
like that of thy breast which sealing thy heart,
opens a blood-stained mouth thirsty to kiss,
one that breathes love. Thy two mouths stiff with
    thirst
of love, the lips curled, are silent. The tongue
in one, the heart in the other, are resting,
parched and dry now for having loved so much.

From thy mouth issued the sayings that are
together fire and freshness; from thy mouth

came the Sermon on the Mount that inspired
the eternal law of eternal love;
the orison of thy lips that gives comfort
for having been born by the pain of death.

MIGUEL DE UNAMUNO
(1864–1936)
Translated from the Spanish by
Eleanor L. Turnbull

Christ Perceived Truly

It is far sweeter to see You born into the world of the Virgin
Mother than to see you born in splendor of the Father before the
morning star; to see you die on the cross, than to see you ruling the
angels in heaven. Nowhere do I perceive Christ more truly than
where He hangs on the cross.

SAINT ANSELM
(1033–1109)

Deep Calls to Deep

Two different dimensions are revealed to us by love when it becomes redemptive: below is the abyss of sin, above the heaven of
the divine goodness lit by the sun of mercy. Deep calls to deep:
the abyss of darkness calls to the abyss of light. The divine love
raises the sinner and makes satisfaction for sin, acting with all the
fullness of its powers by way of mercy. Here God is truly God. It

is pre-eminently by the occasion of sin, the aggressive revolt against the love of God, that this love can manifest itself in all its fullness.

By an unexpected reverse, deriving from the mystery at the heart of the Divinity, it is through an act of exceeding love that God, acting in and through Himself, reveals to us something of His justice, which could not in fact appear in the Person of the Son of God in any other guise than that of love; for in God justice is love.

PÈRE PHILIPPE DE LA TRINITÉ, O.C.D.

(1908–   )

From Quia Amore Langueo

In a valley of this restless mind
    I sought in mountain and in mead,
Trusting a true love for to find.
    Upon an hill then took I heed;
    A voice I heard (and near I yede)[1]
In great dolour complaining tho:
    "See, dear soul, how my sides bleed
        Quia amore langueo."[2]

Upon this hill I found a tree,
    Under a tree a man sitting;
From head to foot wounded was he;
    His heartè blood I saw bleeding:
    A seemly man to be a king,

---

[1] Went, drew.   [2] Because I languish with love.

A gracious face to look unto.
  I askèd why he had paining:—
    "Quia amore langueo.

"I am true love that false was never;
  My sister, man's soul, I loved her thus.
Because we would in no wise dissever
  I left my kingdom glorious.
  I purveyed her a palace full precious;
She fled, I followed, I loved her so
  That I suffered this pain piteous
    Quia amore langueo.

"My fair love and my spouse bright!
  I saved her from beating, and she hath me bet;[3]
I clothed her in grace and heavenly light;
  This bloody shirt she hath on me set;
  For longing of love yet would I not let;
Sweetè strokes are thesè: lo!
I have loved her ever as I her het[4]
    Quia amore langueo.

"I crowned her with bliss, and she me with thorn;
  I led her to chamber, and she me to die;
I brought her to worship, and she me to scorn;
  I did her reverence, she me villany.
  To love that loveth is no maistry;
Her hate made never my love her foe:
  Askè me then no question why—
    Quia amore langueo.

---

[3] Beat.   [4] Promised.

"Look unto mine handès, man!
    These gloves were given me when I her sought;
They be not white, but red and wan:
    Embroidered with blood my spouse them brought.
    They will not off; I loose hem[5] nought;
I woo her with hem wherever she go.
    These hands for her so friendly fought
        Quia amore langueo.

"Marvel not, man, though I sit still.
    See, love hath shod me wonder strait:
Buckled my feet, as was her will,
    With sharpé nails (well thou may'st wait!).
    In my love was never desait;
All my members I have opened her to;
    My body I made her hertè's bait[6]
        Quia amore langueo.

"In my side I have made her nest;
    Look in, how wet a wound is here!
This is her chamber, here shall she rest,
    That she and I may sleep in fere.[7]
    Here may she wash, if any filth were;
Here is seat for all her woe;
    Come when she will, she shall have cheer
        Quia amore langueo.

"I will abide till she be ready,
    I will her sue if she say nay;

---

[5] Them.   [6] Haven, resting-place.   [7] Together.

If she be reckless[8] I will be greedy,
  If she be dangerous[9] I will her pray;
  If she weep, then bide I ne may:
Mine arms ben spread to clip her me to,
  Cry once, 'I come: now, soul, assay!'
    Quia amore langueo."

ANONYMOUS
(*c.* 1450–1500)

Who Overcame by Good

He is stretched out upon a Cross Who by His word stretched out the heavens. He is held fast in bonds Who has set the sand a bound for the sea. He is given gall to drink Who has given us wells of honey. He is crowned with thorns Who has crowned the earth with flowers. With a reed they struck His Head Who of old struck Egypt with ten plagues, and submerged the head of Pharaoh in the waves. That countenance was spat upon at which the Cherubim dare not gaze. Yet, while suffering these things He prayed for His tormentors, saying: "Father, forgive them, for they know not what they do."

He overcame evil by goodness. Christ undertook the defense of those who put Him to death: eager to gather them into His net; annulling the charge, and pleading their ignorance. Made the sport of their drunken frenzy, He submitted without bitterness. He suffered their drunkenness, and in His love for mankind called them to repentance. What more could He do?

Profiting nothing from that goodness, they enclose Him in a

---

[8] Heedless, indifferent.   [9] Disdainful, unyielding.

tomb Whom creation cannot contain. They seal the tomb, safe-guarding our deliverance; and fearing He would rise again, they station soldiers to watch the sepulchre. Who has ever seen the dead placed under watch? Or rather, who has ever seen a dead body treated as an enemy? Who has ever seen one struck by death causing fear to those who have slain him? Who fears his enemy, once he has killed him? And who will not forget his enmity when sated by the death of his adversary?

SAINT AMPHILOCHIUS
(born *c.* 343)

The Sufferings of the Messiah
Psalm 21

My God, my God, why have You forsaken me,
    far from my prayers, from the sound of my cry?
My God, I cry out by day and You do not answer,
    by night and you do not heed me:
But You dwell in the holy place,
    the praise of Israel.
In You our fathers hoped,
    they hoped and You delivered them:
To You they cried out and they were rescued,
    in You they trusted, and were not put to shame.
But I am a worm, not a man,
    scorned by men, despised by the people:
All those who see me, mock me,
    they open their lips, they nod their heads:
"In the Lord he trusted, let Him free him,
    let Him rescue him if He loves him!"

Yes, You have led me even from the womb,
    made me secure as at my mother's breast:
I was given over to You from the beginning,
    from my mother's womb You have been my God:
Now be not far from me, for I am in anguish,
    be near me, for there is no one to aid me.
Many bulls surround me,
    strong bulls of Basan beset me,
They have opened their mouths wide for me,
    like a lion they rave and roar.
My strength is poured out like water,
    all my bones are out of joint:
My heart is like wax,
    melting away in my breast:
My throat is dry like baked clay,
           my tongue sticks to my mouth,
    You have brought me down to the dust of death.
See, many dogs surround me,
    a band of evil men closes in on me:
They have pierced my hands and my feet,
    I can count all my bones.
But they stare and gloat over me,
         they divide my garments among them,
    they cast lots for my clothing.
But You, O Lord, be not far off,
    O my strength, hasten to help me!
Deliver my soul from the sword,
    my life from the hold of the dog:
Save me from the mouth of the lion,
    defend me from the horns of wild bulls.

KING DAVID
(died *c.* 973 B.C.)

The Killing

That was the day they killed the Son of God
On a squat hill-top by Jerusalem.
Zion was bare, her children from their maze
Sucked by the demon curiosity
Clean through the gates. The very halt and blind
Had somehow got themselves up to the hill.

After the ceremonial preparation,
The scourging, nailing, nailing against the wood,
Erection of the main-trees with their burden,
While from the hill rose an orchestral wailing,
They were there at last, high up in the soft spring day.
We watched the writhings, heard the moanings, saw
The three heads turning on their separate axles
Like broken wheels left spinning. Round *his* head
Was loosely bound a crown of plaited thorn
That hurt at random, stinging temple and brow
As the pain swung into its envious circle.
In front the wreath was gathered in a knot
That as he gazed looked like the last stump left
Of a death-wounded deer's great antlers. Some
Who came to stare grew silent as they looked,
Indignant or sorry. But the hardened old
And the hard-hearted young, although at odds
From the first morning, cursed him with one curse,
Having prayed for a Rabbi or an armed Messiah
And found the Son of God. What use to them
Was a God or a Son of God? Of what avail
For purposes such as theirs? Beside the cross-foot,

Alone, four women stood and did not move
All day. The sun revolved, the shadow wheeled,
The evening fell. His head lay on his breast,
But in his breast they watched his heart move on
By itself alone accomplishing its journey.
Their taunts grew louder, sharpened by the knowledge
That he was walking in the park of death,
Far from their rage. Yet all grew stale at last,
Spite, curiosity, envy, hate itself.
They waited only for death and death was slow
And came so quietly they scarce could mark it.
They were angry then with death and death's deceit.

I was a stranger, could not read these people
Or this outlandish deity. Did a God
Indeed in dying cross my life that day
By chance, he on his road and I on mine?

EDWIN MUIR
(1887–1959)

Flower and Fruit

Your wounds, my Jesus,
are my delight, my whole good,
and yet they break my heart.

They are clefts in that divine rock
where love looks out
to make a nest for the dove, flying listlessly.

They are portals to the pool of mercy,
ports of entry to salvation;
and yet they break my heart.

They are five roses on a red rosebush widening;
five pomegranates cleaved wide
on the wide-pierced trunk of a pomegranate tree.
They are flower and fruit
of the Promised Land,
and yet they break my heart.

They are the wounds of a captain
gone ahead to spy out the land,
the wounds given you
in the good fight to save all the rest.
They are the wounds of a lover
who declares his passion;
and yet they break my heart.

They are the wounds you chose
to accept for men—
in your hands, that they might not wound;
in your feet, so they could not run away;
in your heart, to open the pardon door;[1]
and yet they break my heart.

JOSÉ DE VALDIVIELSO
(1560?–1638)
*Translated from the Spanish by
Sister M. Katharine Elaine, C.S.C.*

---

[1] An inner door in some of the medieval cathedrals, kept closed to public penitents until their reconciliation with God.

In Praise of Death in Christ

O Love, now have enough, now set thyself some bounds, since my Jesus hangeth dead before thy eyes! He is dead, He is proven to be dead, that I may have life more abundantly. He is dead, that I might live more happily.

O dearest death of Christ, thou art my happiest possession. I beg thee, let my soul find a nest for itself in thee, O death! O death, thou bringest forth the fruits of eternal life. Let the life-giving floods that flow from thee, I beg thee, overwhelm me. O death, thou art eternal life; I beg thee, let me ever hope beneath thy wings. O wholesome death, let my soul, I beg thee, dwell amid thy glorious blessings. O most precious death, thou art the dearest thing I own. I beg thee, engulf my whole life in thyself and immerse my death in thee.

O most efficacious death of Christ, let my death, I pray thee, be safe and tranquil under thy protection. O life-giving death, let me melt away beneath thy wings. O glorious death! O fruitful death! O death, the sum of all salvation, thou art the beloved covenant of my redemption, the firm pact of my reconciliation! O triumphant, sweet, and life-giving death, in thee shineth forth such great charity towards me that its like is not found in heaven or on earth.

SAINT GERTRUDE
(1256–1302?)

The Crucifixion as Glory

He . . . called the crucifixion "glory" to teach us that there is nothing so base and ignominious that it does not make the one who endures it shine more splendidly—when he endures it for God's sake. In fact, after Judas had gone out to betray Him, He said: "Now is the Son of Man glorified," by this means dispelling the gloomy reflections of the disciples and persuading them not only not to be downcast, but even to rejoice. That is why He kept rebuking Peter from the start[1] because it is a great glory for Him who has come into the power of death to win a victory over death.

SAINT JOHN CHRYSOSTOM
(345?–407)

My Victorious King

My victorious King receives his vestments from mocking
Men at arms, but he is dressed inwardly
In a red royal tunic—so as conqueror
Of evil, prince of right, he stands in glory.
May I cry for him, for the purple and red,
That they might flow from me as tears
Yielding meaning, distilled from my contemplation
So that my being becomes a spring of his mystery.
Our sins are his color, lamb's wool
Stained red by the Father,
And so as Christ takes him as prince, he takes us,
And suffers them. O Christ, Holy Lamb, please hide
My red sins, hell's faggots for fire,
In my King's redeeming royalty.

JEAN DE LA CEPPÈDE
(1550–1622)
Translated from the French by
Clinton Larson

---

[1] When he protested at Christ's predictions of the Passion.

'Fill High the Bowl'

'Fill high the bowl, and spice it well, and pour
    The dews oblivious: for the Cross is sharp,
      The Cross is sharp, and He
      Is tenderer than a lamb.

'He wept by Lazarus' grave—how will He bear
This bed of anguish? and His pale weak form
      Is worn with many a watch
      Of sorrow and unrest.

'His sweat last night was as great drops of blood,
And the sad burthen press'd Him so to earth,
      The very torturers paus'd
      To help Him on His way.

'Fill high the bowl, benumb His aching sense
With medicin'd sleep.'—O awful in Thy woe!
      The parching thirst of death
      Is on Thee, and Thou triest

The slumb'rous potion bland, and wilt not drink:
Not sullen, nor in scorn, like haughty man
      With suicidal hand
      Putting his solace by:

But as at first Thine all-pervading look
Saw from Thy Father's bosom to th' abyss,
      Measuring in calm presage
      The infinite descent;

So to the end, though now of mortal pangs
Made heir, and emptied of Thy glory awhile,

With unaverted eye
Thou meetest all the storm.

Thou wilt feel all, that Thou mayst pity all;
And rather wouldst Thou wrestle with strong pain,
　　Than overcloud Thy soul,
　　So clear in agony,

Or lose one glimpse of heaven before the time.
O most entire and perfect sacrifice,
　　Renew'd in every pulse
　　That on the tedious Cross

Told the long hours of death, as, one by one,
The life-strings of that tender heart gave way;
　　E'en sinners, taught by Thee,
　　Look sorrow in the face,

And bid her freely welcome, unbeguil'd
By false kind solaces, and spells of earth:—
　　And yet not all unsooth'd
　　For when was joy so dear,

As the deep calm that breath'd *Father, forgive,*
Or, *'Be with Me in paradise to-day'*?
　　And, though the strife be sore,
　　Yet in His parting breath

Love masters agony; the soul that seem'd
Forsaken, feels her present God again,
　　And in her Father's arms
　　Contented dies away.

JOHN KEBLE
(1792–1866)

On the Crucifixion

It was but now their sounding clamours sung,
Blessed is he, that comes from the most high,
And all the mountains with Hosanna rung,
And now, away with him, away they cry,
And nothing can be heard but crucify:
    It was but now, the crown itself they save,
    And golden name of king unto him gave,
And now, no king, but only Caesar, they will have:

It was but now they gathered blooming May,
And of his arms disrob'd the branching tree,
To strew with boughs, and blossoms all thy way,
And now, the branchless trunk a cross for thee,
And May, dismayed, thy coronet must be:
    It was but now they were so kind, to throw
    Their own best garments, where thy feet should go,
And now, thyself they strip, and bleeding wounds they show.

See where the author of all life is dying:
O fearful day! he dead, what hope of living?
See where the hopes of all our lives are buying:
O cheerful day! they bought, what fear of grieving?
Love love for hate and death for life is giving:
    Lo how his arms are stretch'd abroad to grace thee,
    And, as they open stand, call to embrace thee,
Why stay'st thou then my soul; O fly, fly, thither haste thee.

GILES FLETCHER
(1588?–1623)

Crucifying

By miracles exceeding power of man,
He faith in some, envy in some begat,
For, what weak spirits admire, ambitious, hate;
In both affections many to him ran,
But oh! the worst are most, they will and can,
Alas, and do, unto the immaculate,
Whose creature fate is, now prescribe a fate,
Measuring self-lifes infinity to'a span,
Nay to an inch. Lo, where condemned he
Bears his own cross, with pain, yet by and by
When it bears him, he must bear more and die.
Now thou art lifted up, draw me to thee,
And at thy death giving such liberal dole,
Moist, with one drop of thy blood, my dry soul.

JOHN DONNE
(1573–1631)

Casting All Your Care Upon God, for He Careth for You

Come, heavy souls, oppressed that are
With doubts, and fears, and carking care.
Lay all your burthens down, and see
Where's One that carried once a tree
Upon His back, and, which is more,

A heavier weight, your sins, He bore.
Think then how easily He can
Your sorrows bear that's God and Man;
Think too how willing He's to take
Your care on Him, Who for your sake
Sweat bloody drops, prayed, fasted, cried,
Was bound, scourged, mocked and crucified
He that so much for you did do,
Will do yet more, and care for you.

THOMAS WASHBOURNE
(1606–1687)

Give Me To Drink

Of all our Lord's physical sufferings, only one, "I thirst," rose to
His lips.

WILLA CATHER
(1873–1947)

Sitio: The Thirst of Christ

At the end, we are told, we shall be judged on love. That is why
the thirst of God is not only awful but lovely and consoling as well.
If we try to humble and to open our hearts to love, then we need
not fear. We are weak and therefore we sin; and sometimes we

sin in a far worse way, becoming hard and rebellious and giving ourselves deliberately to evil; but always there is forgiveness, even to seventy times seven, if we turn again to God in humility and love. . . .

If we hesitate at the paradox of a love which is at once so fierce and so gentle, so devouring and so patient, there is the figure of Christ on the Cross to keep us from shrinking from the fierceness, to re-assure us as again and again in the pages of the Gospel he re-assures us, fear not, and to show us in the agony of his own body how the fire of divine love is a fire that first of all devours the heart of God. . . .

How then can we fear the thirst of God? And yet we continue in fact to flee him down the arches of the years: why? Because in our blindness we prefer the labyrinthine ways of our own egoism: we know that to love is to give, to love totally is to give totally, and we fear the loss of our own self-hood: never more to be able to arrange things for ourselves (as though we ever could), never more to feel that we are the masters of our fate . . . And so we miss the fire, we miss the fullness of life, we miss the real freedom. That is why Good Friday is not just an event in the past but something that is to be done in us every day: that going down into the deep places where we see ourselves for what we really are, see reality as it is, that leaving of the conventional religious shallows to plunge into the ocean of love, that companionship of Christ on the Cross that teaches us to say with him his final word: *In manus tuas*: into thy hands. . . . That is the acceptance of reality; that is the gateway to life. Into thy hands, O Lord, I commend this joy, this sorrow, this problem, this decision; into thy hands I commend each moment as it comes, each event as thou sendest it to me; into thy hands I put this thing I have to do or suffer; into thy hands I commend my life as a whole, all that I am: be it done to me according to thy word—that is the thing that is asked of us. And if we are trying to do this we need not fear; and if in the end we can succeed in doing it wholly and gladly we shall have shared fully in the *In manus tuas* of Christ, and so we shall be able to share also in his *Consummatum est:* we shall have learnt fully the meaning of love, and so, with Christ in his glory, we shall have come home.

GERALD VANN
(1906–1963)

The Little Hill

Oh, here the air is sweet and still,
    And soft's the grass to lie on;
And far away's the little hill
    They took for Christ to die on.

And there's a hill across the brook,
    And down the brook's another;
But, oh, the little hill they took,—
    I think I am its mother!

The moon that saw Gethsemane,
    I watch it rise and set;
It has so many things to see,
    They help it to forget.

But little hills that sit at home
    So many hundred years,
Remember Greece, remember Rome,
    Remember Mary's tears.

And far away in Palestine,
    Sadder than any other,

Grieves still the hill that I call mine,—
I think I am its mother.

EDNA ST. VINCENT MILLAY
(1892–1950)

The Everlasting Cry

. . . If the Son of Man, in his very last hour,
Cried out louder than a lost soul in his dreadful anguish,
With a cry that rang as untrue as a divine blasphemy,
It was because the Son of God knew.

One wonders why he should have uttered that dreadful cry.
One wonders, had it been otherwise.

All the statements are positive, at that moment he uttered a
dreadful cry.

So one wonders why at that moment he should have uttered
that dreadful cry.

On the contrary. He should have been pleased.

It was over.

It was done.

All was finished.

His passion was at an end; his incarnation was as it were at
an end; achieved; his passion was completed; achieved; redemption
was completed; achieved.

There was nothing left (for him) but that formality: death.

Redemption was completed and crowned;

Crowned with thorns, the supreme crown.

It was at that moment that he should; that he ought to have
been happy.

O best beloved son who went back to his father;
Son of tender love who went up again to heaven;
Son among all sons who went home to his father,
Prodigal child, son prodigal of his blood;
O best beloved son who went up to his father.

One wonders why he should have cried out at that moment.
He had precisely begun to make an end.
  He had served his time of humanity;
He was leaving the prison for the home of glory;
He was returning to his father's house.

Like a traveler at the last hours of his journey,
He had finished his journey on earth;
He had ended his journey to Jerusalem.

Like a tired traveler at the last hours of his journey, He saw
his home.

And like a reaper at the end of his day,
In both his father's hands he poured out his pay;
Like a tired reaper at the end of his harvest;
In both his father's hands he poured out his pay,
The souls of the just he had redeemed,
The pay he had so hardly earned.
  The souls of the saints he had sanctified.
The souls of the just he had justified.
And the souls of sinners that he had justified with one and the
  other hand.
That he had picked up like an ear of grain on the ground.
That he had justified by his merits. . . .
He was like a son at the last hours of his day;
His father was waiting for him to embrace him at last;

An eternal kiss would lave his unsullied side;
A fatherly kiss would lave his unsullied brow;
An eternal kiss from his father would lave his smarting wounds,
Would refresh his smarting wounds,
And his head, and his side, and his feet, and his hands.
An eternal spring, pure eternal water awaited his smarting
wounds. . . .

As he was going to return to his eternity,
On the point of returning into his eternity,
It is then all the statements agree, all the statements are positive,
it is then he uttered that awful cry. . . .

Cry still ringing in all humanity;
Cry that made the Church militant totter;
In which the suffering Church too recognized its own fear;
Through which the Church triumphant experienced its triumph;
Cry ringing at the heart of all humanity;
Cry ringing at the heart of all Christendom;
O culminating cry, everlastingly valid.

Cry as if God himself had sinned like us;
As if God himself had despaired;
O culminating cry, everlastingly valid.

As if even God had sinned like us.
Committing the greatest sin.
Which is to despair.
The sin of despair.

Louder than the two thieves hanging beside him;
And who howled at death like famished dogs.
The thieves howled but a human howl;

The thieves howled but a cry of human death;
Also they slavered but human slaver:

The Just One alone uttered the everlasting cry.

CHARLES PÉGUY
(1873–1914)
Translated from the French by
Julian Green

Daybreak

The storm lies collapsed but quivering still
At the pallid rim of heaven.
The sick man thinks, "Now it is day, and I'll sleep,"
As he presses his febrile lids shut.
The calf in the stall reaches out with strong nostrils
To fill them with early morning air.
In the silent wood an unwashed tramp
Gets up from his easy bed of last year's leaves.
With insolent hand he throws the nearest stone
At a pigeon flying by half asleep,
Then shivers as the stone, too heavy,
Falls to the ground with a thud.
The stream courses on as if to overtake night
In its stealthy flight into darkness.
Wildly, on and on, with cold breath, rushes the heedless
water
While over it, on the little bridge,
Jesus and his mother speak softly.
Softly, softly they speak, yet indestructible as stars
Are their words, their dialogue brief and eternal.
He bears his cross, and says merely, "My mother!"

As he looks at her, she replies, "O my Son!"
Heaven holds converse, weighed down and silent, with
  earth;
And earth, while a shudder goes through her age-old body,
Rallies to live the new day.
Light, early and spectral, is dawning.
Someone is stealing, without his shoes, from a woman's bed.
Like a shadow he runs,
Then climbs like a thief through a window
Into his own room.
Seeing himself in the mirror, he suddenly fears this pale
  stranger
Who during a sleepless night has murdered the innocent
  lad
He once was, and who now in derision comes back
To wash his hands in the bowl of his victim—
And all as if this explained why the heavens were heavy,
And everything estranged in earth's air.
Now the door to the stable is opened.
Now it is really day.

HUGO VON HOFMANNSTHAL
(1874–1929)
Translated from the German by
Frida Grosser

At the Heart of the World

The cross is God at work. It is not only His instrument, it is His
active form, His extracting unifying operation, His extension
between the four cardinal points: the north or zenith which is the
root in the *firmament*; the south or nadir which is matter warmed

by grace on which force is exerted; the arms to the right and the left are the instruments of His temporal energy.

Thus it is not only of the creature that one can say, as Saint Paul does (Rom. viii.22), that *the whole of nature . . . groans in a common travail all the while.* It is of the Creator Himself (similar to Samson in the power of the Philistines, deposed and "put to work"). . . . That is what keeps the mass of surrounding things from being at rest, that is what torments them and secretly upsets them in their balance. [The cross] is a solicitation revealed in an ever expanding area by all kinds of swellings, explosions, ebbings, destructions, and also by momentary coalitions and trials in an attitude of resistance, but soon reduced by an innate incoherence and the irresistible temptation of weight. Since God was crucified in the middle of everything, the world now is concerned only with paying attention deliberately to that heart which beats and attracts it.

PAUL CLAUDEL
(1868–1955)

Means and End

The Christian message is not a prophecy of condemnation. It calls to penance in order to call to salvation. It is not bitter; it is not ill-tempered; it is not discourteous; it is not ironic; it is not pessimistic. It is generous. It is strong and joyful. It is full of beauty and poetry. It is full of vigor and majesty. Indeed, it raises the Cross: suffering, sacrifice, death, but to bring comfort, redemption, life.

POPE PAUL VI
(1897–   )

Good Friday

Am I a stone, and not a sheep,
    That I can stand, O Christ, beneath Thy cross,
    To number drop by drop Thy Blood's slow loss,
And yet not weep?

Not so those women loved
    Who with exceeding grief lamented Thee;
    Not so fallen Peter weeping bitterly;
Not so the thief was moved;

Not so the Sun and Moon
    Which hid their faces in a starless sky.
    A horror of great darkness at broad noon—
I, only I.

Yet give not o'er,
    But seek Thy sheep, true Shepherd of the flock;
    Greater than Moses, turn and look once more
And smite a rock.

CHRISTINA ROSSETTI
(1830–1894)

Pietà
From The Life of the Virgin Mary

Now is my misery full, and namelessly
it fills me. I am stark, as the stone's
inside is stark.

Hard as I am, I know but one thing:
You grew—
. . . and grew
in order to stand forth
as too great pain
quite beyond my heart's grasping.
Now you are lying straight across my lap,
now I can no longer give you birth.

RAINER MARIA RILKE
(1875–1926)
Translated from the German by
M. D. Herter Norton

The Untilled Paradise

O Mother of God, thou art the mystical paradise, which, untilled, produced Christ, through whom that life-bearing tree, the Cross, is planted on earth. Wherefore we now adore its exaltation, and magnify thee.

NINTH ODE AT MATINS[1]
BYZANTINE MENAEA
(8th century)

Courage To Die

This Cross of Christ, on which the whole light of revelation is centered, is, too, the only possible key to the meaning of human

---

[1] Feast of the Exaltation of the Holy Cross, September 14.

history, whether profane—or appears to be so—or sacred. The cross of Christ, and it alone, is capable of unravelling the experience of mankind, both of each individual and of the whole human race. And the cross of Christ, let us make no mistake about it, involves our own. Christ died on the cross to save us, but that does not mean he died to save us from the necessity of dying. He died, rather, to give us courage to die as well, to help us to do so, to enable us to die in very deed. "If we suffer with him," says St. Paul, "we shall be also glorified with him" (Rom. viii.17). "If we be dead with him, we shall live with him. If we suffer, we shall also reign with him" (II Tim. ii.12). Baptism, as he interprets it, engrafts us in Christ's death, so that we may share, as well, in his resurrection.

LOUIS BOUYER
(1913–   )

Good Friday: the Third Nocturne

Alone to sacrifice Thou goest, Lord,
Giving Thyself to death whom Thou hast slain.
For us Thy wretched folk is any word,
Who know that for our sins this is Thy pain?

For they are ours, O Lord, our deeds, our deeds,
Why must Thou suffer torture for our sin?
Let our hearts suffer for Thy passion, Lord,
That sheer compassion may Thy mercy win.

This is that night of tears, the three days' space,
Sorrow abiding of the eventide,

Until the day break with the risen Christ,
And hearts that sorrowed shall be satisfied.

So may our hearts have pity on Thee, Lord,
That they may sharers of Thy glory be:
Heavy with weeping may the three days pass,
To win the laughter of Thine Easter Day.

PETER ABELARD
(1079–1142)
Translated from the Latin by
Helen Waddell

My Daughter on Good Friday

Suddenly it must have seemed, in the hovering and still day,
Someone impressive had died. Our next door neighbors had gone
   away

On their yearly visit, and she swung on their little girl's swing,
But let her swinging die down to stillness. She appeared listening

For some companionable voice, but heard just the little birds
Cry weep! weep! from the tall aspen leaves, in the place of words.

Concerning the rest of us, we herded round our things
Of kitchen and parlor, and watched Rachel watching murmurings.

As for the death, it was long, long ago; so long, it seems, that
We are not really sure it was, nor is it real as Rachel's ribboned hat

Blowing back over the landscape, that's ferny with the billion times
Of birth and death, death and birth, now, as Rachel climbs.

SHELDON TANNENBAUM
(1929–   )

In Holy Week

Around us still the dark of night
And still so early in the world
That stars unnumbered range the sky,
Each shining with the day's clear light,
And if it could the earth upcurled
Would wearily through Easter-tide
Sleep to the chanting of the Psalms.

Around us still the dark of night
And still so early in the world
That like eternity the square
Corner to crossroad is unfurled
And dawn and warmth are out of sight
More than a thousand years away.

And still the earth in nakedness
Has naught to wear by night to ring
The chapel bell out in response
To where inside the choirs sing.

And from Thursday of Holy Week
Till Holy Saturday begins
The water ploughs the river banks
And in its eddying whirlpools spins.

Stripped down and bare the forest rears,
And when Christ's Passion comes to pass
Its host of lofty pine-trees stand
Like worshippers attending Mass
And in the town where like a rally
They crowd together down the ways,
The trees in their pure nakedness
In through the church's gratings gaze.

And awe transfixes all their glances,
Alarm that you may well forgive,
For gardens burst out through their fences
And earth's foundations quake and move
And God is borne into the grave.

They see the light, the royal gate,
The rows of candles, the black pall,
The faces deeply stained with tears:
But suddenly before them all
A concourse with the shroud appears;
Two birches standing at the gate
Must bow aside to let them pass.

Round the yard goes the procession
And back along the pavement's edge,
To bear the spring, spring's conversation
Along the street into the porch,
And air with flavours of baked bread
And heady vapours of the spring.

Now March is scattering the snow
On groups of cripples in the porch
As though someone had brought the shrine

Outside, and to them, each and each,
Had given all he could bestow.

So lasts the singing till the dawn.
And when they cease their lengthy weep
The Psalms and Acts on silent feet
Now in the stillness softly creep
Into an empty, lamplit street.

And men and beasts at midnight hush
To hear this rumour in the spring,
That in the changing weather's hour
Death finds its only vanquishing
Through the Resurrection's power.

BORIS PASTERNAK
(1890–1960)
Translated from the Russian by
Henry Kamen

This Most Beautiful Tree

Divine Love crossed the infinity of space and time to come from God to us. But how can it repeat the journey in the opposite direction, starting from a finite creature? When the seed of divine love placed in us has grown and become a tree, how can we, who bear it, take it back to its origin? How can we repeat the journey made by God when he came to us, in the opposite direction? How can we cross infinite distance?

It seems impossible, but there is a way,—a way with which we are familiar. We know quite well in what likeness this tree is made, this tree that has grown within us, this most beautiful tree where the birds of the air come and perch. We know what is the most beautiful of all trees. "No forest bears its equal." Something still a little more frightful than a gibbet—that is the most beautiful of all trees. It was the seed of this tree that God placed within us, without our knowing what seed it was. If we had known, we should not have said yes at the first moment. It is this tree that has grown within us and has become ineradicable. Only a betrayal can uproot it.

When we hit a nail with a hammer, the whole of the shock received by the large head of the nail passes into the point without any of it being lost, although it is only a point. If the hammer and the head of the nail were infinitely big it would be just the same. The point of the nail would transmit this infinite shock at the point to which it was applied.

Extreme affliction, which means physical pain, distress of soul, and social degradation, all at the same time, is a nail whose point is applied at the very center of the soul, whose head is all necessity spreading throughout space and time. . . .

He whose soul remains ever turned toward God though the nail pierces it finds himself nailed to the very center of the universe. It is the true center; it is not in the middle; it is beyond space and time; it is God. In a dimension that does not belong to space, that is not time, that is indeed quite a different dimension, this nail has pierced cleanly through all creation, through the thickness of the screen separating the soul from God.

In this marvelous dimension, the soul, without leaving the place and the instant where the body to which it is united is situated, can cross the totality of space and time and come into the very presence of God.

It is at the intersection of creation and its Creator. This point of intersection is the point of intersection of the arms of the Cross.

Saint Paul was perhaps thinking about things of this kind when he said, "That ye, being rooted and grounded in love, may be able to comprehend with all saints what is the breadth, and length, and depth, and height; and to know the love of Christ, which passeth knowledge."[1]

SIMONE WEIL
(1909–1943)

The End of all Ends

The bridal union of the soul with God is the end for which the soul was created, bought by the Cross, accomplished on the Cross, and sealed with the Cross for all eternity.

EDITH STEIN[2]
(1891–1942)

[1] Eph. iii.17-19.
[2] Edith Stein was a German philosopher and Jewess who became a Carmelite nun in Holland. She was taken from her convent and murdered in a Nazi gas chamber.

III

THE MYSTERY
AT THE CORE

Lord, what is man? why should he cost Thee
So dear? what had his ruin lost Thee?
Lord, what is man, that Thou has over-bought
So much a thing of naught?

RICHARD CRASHAW
(1612?–1649)

LETTERS CONCERNING
THE MYSTERY

I

On me, least as I am of all the saints, he has bestowed this privilege, of making known to the Gentiles the unfathomable riches of Christ, of publishing to the world the plan of this mystery, kept hidden from the beginning of time in the all-creating mind of God. (To the Ephesians, 3:8-10)

II

What has become of the wise men, the scribes, the philosophers of this age we live in? Must we not say that God has turned our worldly wisdom to folly? When God shewed us his wisdom; the world, with all its wisdom, could not find its way to God; and now God would use a foolish thing, our preaching, to save those who will believe in it. Here are the Jews asking for signs and wonders, here are the Greeks intent on their philosophy; but what we preach is Christ crucified; to the Jews, a discouragement, to the Gentiles, mere folly; but to us who have been called, Jew and Gentile alike, Christ the power of God, Christ the wisdom of God. So much wiser than men is God's foolishness; so much stronger than men is God's weakness. (To the Corinthians, I, 1:20-25)

III

In the Son of God, in his blood, we find the redemption that sets us free from our sins. He is the true likeness of the God we cannot see; his is that first birth which precedes every act of creation. Yes, in him all created things took their being, heavenly and earthly, visible and invisible; what are thrones and dominions, what are princedoms and powers? They were all created through him and in him; he takes precedency of all, and in him all subsist. . . . Thus in every way the primacy was to become his. It was God's good pleasure to let all completeness dwell in him, and through him to win back all things, whether on earth or in heaven, into union with himself, making peace with them through his blood, shed on the cross. (*To the Colossians*, 1:14-20)

I V

He did not raise himself to the dignity of the high priesthood; it was God that raised him to it, when he said, Thou art my Son, I have begotten thee this day, and so, elsewhere, Thou art a priest for ever, in the line of Melchisedech. Christ, during his earthly life, offered prayer and entreaty to the God who could save him from death, not without a piercing cry, not without tears; yet with such piety as won him a hearing. Son of God though he was, he learned obedience in the school of suffering, and now, his full achievement reached, he wins eternal salvation for all those who render obedience to him. (*To the Hebrews*, 5:5-10)

V

Yours is to be the same mind which Christ Jesus shewed. His nature is, from the first, divine, and yet he did not see, in the rank of Godhead, a prize to be coveted; he dispossessed himself, and took the nature of a slave, fashioned in the likeness of men, and presenting himself to us in human form; and then he lowered his own dignity, accepted an obedience which brought him to death, death *on a cross. That is why God has raised him to such a height, given him that name which is greater than any other name; so that everything in heaven and on earth and under the earth must bend the knee before the name of Jesus, and every tongue must confess Jesus Christ as the Lord, dwelling in the glory of God the Father. (To the Philippians, 2:5-11)*

SAINT PAUL
(martyred *c.* 67 A.D.)

Both Man and God

If He was not a man, who was beaten with blows? And if He were not God, who healed the ear which Peter had cut off, and who restored it to its place?

If He was not a man, whose face was spat upon? And if He were not God, who breathed the Holy Spirit upon the faces of the Apostles?

If He was not a man, who was it stood before Pilate at the judgement seat? And if He were not God, who caused the wife of Pilate to suffer many things in a dream?

If He was not a man, upon whose garments did the soldiers cast lots, dividing them amongst them? And if He were not God, for what reason did the sun grow dark above the Cross?

If He was not a man, who was it hung upon a cross? And if He were not God, who moved the earth from its foundations?

If He was not a man, whose hands were pierced by the nails? And if He were not God, how was the veil of the temple rent in two, and the rocks split asunder, and the graves opened?

If He was not a man, who cried out, "My God, My God, why hast Thou abandoned me"? And if He were not God, who then hath said, "Father, forgive them, for they know not what they do"?

If He was not man, who hung with thieves upon a cross? And if He were not God, for what cause did He say, "This day thou shalt be with me in paradise"?

If He was not man, to whom did they offer gall and vinegar? And if He were not God, at whose voice did they shake and tremble?

If He was not a man, whose side was opened by a lance, and then came out blood and water? And if He were not God, who hath broken the gates of hell, and burst the iron bars? And by whose command did the dead that slept in their graves come forth?

If He was not a man, whom did the Apostles behold in the Upper Room? And if He was not God, in what manner did He enter, the doors being closed?

If He was not a man, in whose hand did Thomas feel the wounds of the nails and the lance? And if He was not God to whom did Thomas cry out saying, "My Lord and My God"?

SAINT EPHRAEM
(306?-373)

King and Servant

Among all the works of God, before which the mind grows faint with awe, which so rejoices yet overwhelms the soul as the Passion of our Saviour? For as often as we dwell, as best we can, upon His Omnipotence, which He shares with the Father in one and the same nature, more wondrous does His lowliness seem to us than His power; and with more difficulty do we grasp His emptying Himself of the divine Majesty, than His sublime uplifting in the form of a servant. Yet it helps us greatly to understand that while One is the Creator, one the created—One the inviolable Divinity, one the suffering flesh—what belongs to either nature meets in the single Person: so that whether in might or in suffering, His the humiliation Whose also [is] the glory.

POPE SAINT LEO THE GREAT
(390?-461)

Barabbas Ponders
From *Barabbas*

There wasn't anyone who rose from the dead, either their adored "Master" or anyone else! And besides, he, Barabbas, could hardly be blamed for their choice. That was their business. They could have chosen anyone at all, but it just turned out that way. The son of God! As if he could be the son of God! But supposing he were, there was surely no need for him to have been crucified if he had not wanted to be. He must have wanted it himself! There was something weird and horrid about it—he must have *wanted* to suffer. For if he really was the son of God, it would have been the easiest thing in the world to get out of it. But he didn't *want* to get out of it. He wanted to suffer and die in that dreadful way and not be spared; and so it had been; he had got his own way about not being let off. He had let him, Barabbas, go free instead. He had commanded:—Release Barabbas and crucify me.

Though of course he was not the son of God, that was obvious ...

He had used his power in the most extraordinary way. Used it by not using it, as it were; allowed others to decide exactly as they liked; refrained from interfering and yet had got his own way all the same: to be crucified instead of Barabbas.

They spoke of his having died for them. That might be. But he really had died for Barabbas, no one could deny it! In actual fact, he was closer to him than they were, closer than anyone else, was bound up with him in quite another way. Although they didn't want to have anything to do with him. He was chosen, one might say, chosen to escape suffering, to be let off. He was the real chosen one, acquitted instead of the son of God himself—at his command, because he wished it. Though they suspected nothing!

But he didn't care for their "brotherhood" and their "love feasts" and their "love one another." He was himself. In his relationship to that crucified man they called the son of God he was also himself, as always. He was no serf under him as they were. Not one of those who went around sighing and praying to him.

How can one *want* to suffer, when there's no need, when one's not forced to? That sort of thing is beyond belief and the mere thought of it almost enough to turn the stomach.

PÄR LAGERKVIST

(1891–   )

Not Robbery To Be Divine

In the sense of the Apostolic witness the Crucifixion of Jesus Christ is the concrete deed and action of God Himself. God changes Himself, God Himself comes most near, God thinks it not robbery to be divine, that is, He does not hold on to the booty like a robber, but God parts with Himself. Such is the glory of His Godhead, that He can be "selfless," that He can actually forgive Himself something. He remains genuinely true to Himself, but just through not having to limit Himself to His Godhead. It is the depth of the Godhead, the greatness of His glory which is revealed in the very fact that it can also completely hide itself in its sheer opposite, in the profoundest rejection and the greatest misery of the creature. What takes place in the Crucifixion of Christ is that God's Son takes to Himself that which must come to the creature existing in revolt, which wants to deliver itself from its creatureliness and itself be the Creator. He puts Himself into this creature's need and does not abandon it to itself. Moreover, He does not only help it from without and greet it only from afar off; He makes the misery of His creatures His own. To what end? So that His creature may go out freely, so that the burden which it has laid upon itself may be borne, borne away. The creature itself must have gone to pieces, but God does not want that; He wants it to be saved. So great is the ruin of the creature that less than the self-surrender of God would not suffice for its rescue. But so great is God, that it is His will to render up Himself. Reconciliation means God taking man's place. Let me add that no doctrine of this central mystery can exhaustively and precisely grasp and express the extent to which God has intervened for us here. Do not confuse my theory of the reconciliation with the thing itself. All theories of reconciliation can be but pointers. But do also pay attention to this "for us": nothing must be deducted from it! Whatever a doctrine of reconciliation tries to express, it *must* say this.

KARL BARTH
(1886–   )

In Habit Found as a Man

It is clear . . . that the passion of Christ is abundantly efficacious to exhaust all sins of every kind (Heb. ix.28). But how can I be sure that it has been offered for me? Most certainly it has been offered for me, because it could not have been offered for anyone else. Might it not have been offered for the angels, perhaps you will say? But the angels had no need of it. Or for the demons? But they had no capacity to avail of it. Hence it is written, "He (Christ Jesus) emptied Himself, taking the form of a servant, being made in the likeness—not of the angels, nor (God forbid!) of the demons, but—of men, and in habit found as a man" (Phil. ii.7).

He was by nature the Son and He made Himself a servant. And not only did He assume the form of a servant in order that He might bear the yoke with us, but He assumed the form of a wicked servant in order that He might suffer in our stead, of the "servant of sin" in order to pay the penalty of sin, whereas in Him sin had no place. Notice how the Apostle does not say, "in the likeness of man" but "in the likeness of men." The reason is, because the first man was created neither in the reality of sinful flesh nor "in the likeness of sinful flesh" (Rom. vii.3), whereas Christ willed to immerse Himself truly and profoundly in all our human miseries, so that the devil's keen eye might not be able to discover that "great mystery of godliness" (I Tim. iii.16). "In habit," therefore, and in every habit, He was "found as a man," nor in what belonged to His human nature, did He appear in anything distinguished from the rest of men. It was indeed because He was so completely "in habit found as a man" that He was crucified. He manifested His divinity to a few in order that there might be some who believed, but to the rest He remained hidden, "for if they had known, they would never have crucified the Lord of glory" (I Cor. ii.8). Another reason why He thus associated ignorance to the sin of the deicides was this: in order that such ignorance might afford Him some shadow of an excuse for pardoning them.

SAINT BERNARD OF CLAIRVAUX
(1091–1153)

The Truest of Men

The truest of all men was the Man of Sorrows.

HERMAN MELVILLE
(1819–1891)

It Needed a God

Man was so limited: he hadn't even the ingenuity to invent a new vice: the animals knew as much. It was for this world that Christ died: the more evil you saw and heard about you, the greater glory lay around the death: it was too easy to die for what was good or beautiful, for home or a civilization—it needed a God to die for the half-hearted and the corrupt.

GRAHAM GREENE
(1904-   )

The Divine Image

Jesus said: 'Wouldest thou love one who never died
For thee, or ever die for one who had not died for thee?
And if God dieth not for Man, and giveth not Himself
Eternally for Man, Man could not exist; for Man is Love,
As God is Love: every kindness to another is a little Death
In the Divine Image; nor can Man exist but by Brotherhood.'

WILLIAM BLAKE
(1757-1827)

Ballad of the Goodly Fere

Simon Zelotes speaketh it somewhile after the Crucifixion

Ha' we lost the goodliest fere[1] o' all
For the priests and the gallows tree?
Aye lover he was of brawny men,
O' ships and the open sea.

When they came wi' a host to take Our Man
His smile was good to see,
"First let these go!" quo' our Goodly Fere,
"Or I'll see ye damned!" says he.

Aye he sent us out through the crossed high spears
And the scorn of his laugh rang free,
"Why took ye not me when I walked about
Alone in the town?" says he.

Oh we drunk his "Hale" in the good red wine
When we last made company,
No capon priest was the Goodly Fere
But a man o' men was he.

I ha' seen him drive a hundred men
Wi' a bundle o' cords swung free,
That they took the high and holy house
For their pawn and treasury.

They'll no' get him a' in a book I think
Though they write it cunningly;

---

[1] Mate; companion.

No mouse of the scrolls was the Goodly Fere
But aye loved the open sea.

'If they think they ha' snared our Goodly Fere
They are fools to the last degree.
"I'll go to the feast," quo' our Goodly Fere,
"Though I go to the gallows tree."

"Ye ha' seen me heal the lame and the blind,
And wake the dead," says he,
"Ye shall see one thing to master all:
" 'Tis how a brave man dies on the tree."

A son of God was the Goodly Fere
That bade us his brothers be.
I ha' seen him cow a thousand men.
I have seen him upon the tree.

He cried no cry when they drave the nails
And the blood gushed hot and free,
The hounds of the crimson sky gave tongue
But never a cry cried he.

I ha' seen him cow a thousand men
On the hills o' Galilee,
They whined as he walked out calm between,
Wi' his eyes like the grey o' the sea,

Like the sea that brooks no voyaging
With the winds unleashed and free,
Like the sea that he cowed at Genseret
Wi' twey words spoke' suddenly.

A master of men was the Goodly Fere,
A mate of the wind and sea,

If they think they ha' slain our Goodly Fere
They are fools eternally.

I ha' seen him eat o' the honey-comb
Sin' they nailed him to the tree.

EZRA POUND
(1885–   )

Finished!

At mocking Pilate's orders—strange commands of a strange man
who meant the priests to be confronted with a reminder—a sign
was nailed up on the cross over the head of Jesus, an inscription
in three languages: Latin, Greek, and Aramaic:

"Jesus of Nazareth, the King of the Jews!"

When he heard that this was being done, Caiphas. . . . came
storming into the small blue-walled room with the fireplace, where
Pilate received his visitors.

"Why do you do such a thing as this to us? Don't write 'King
of the Jews'; if you must write anything, write, 'He said, I am
the King of the Jews.' "

Pilate snorted at Caiphas and a leer twisted his thick, loose-
formed mouth. He was through yielding to this popinjay.

"What I have written I have written," said Pilate, and stalked
back to his wife.

"I feel like a vaticide!" he was reported to tell his wife. "I have
killed a prophet."

"Perhaps," lamented his wife, "you are a deicide—perhaps you
have killed a god."

"But who," cried Pilate, the born interrogator, "can possibly kill a god?"

"That," his wife answered, "is your only hope!"

FULTON OURSLER

(1893–1952)

Himself He Cannot Save

He identified Himself with the sinner, much more, with sin itself. The eternal stigmata He received upon the Cross are the wounds made upon Him by sin, which He took upon Himself in its entirety.

For this reason He is also first among the abandoned ones: God, my God, why has Thou forsaken me! But that is the cry that befits the Saviour of our souls! . . . To this point He loved us—to the point of taking upon Himself that abandonment which would be our eternal portion if He had not come to save us.

Should this cry scandalize us as it did the Jews who shook their heads on seeing His distress and reproached Him with His claim of saving the world—He who could not save Himself and come down from His Cross? They did not understand that at this supreme hour when our salvation was being accomplished, the identification of Christ with powerless and sinful humanity was so complete that as a result the very all-powerfulness of His divinity was bound, remitted entirely by the Son into the hands of the Father. This was the hour when Lucifer was vanquished by the absolute dispossession of the Son of God: in which the crucified Word made manifest that not only in His humanity but eternally in His divinity He had received everything from the Father, the perfect source of the procession of the Son, and the Holy Ghost.

RAÏSSA MARITAIN

(1883–1960)

High Harmonies

Certainly, even for Christians, suffering remains the dark side of experience. It is not placed in the clear light of midday. But from the Cross a powerful shaft of light penetrates the dark abyss, cleaving a path through the darkness and revealing enough to make it easier to endure patiently the obscurity which remains . . .

We cannot, like some, more sentimental than rational, say that God shares the suffering of the world He has created. For since suffering is in itself negative, a defect and a frustration of being, it can have no place in Being Absolutely Perfect. Nor would this doctrine Deity, were it tenable, afford any consolation to human suffering. On the contrary, if the Godhead suffered, then suffering would be irremediable, for suffering would belong to ultimate reality. Never could we escape from suffering to pure bliss. Because, in fact, God is pure bliss, He can and will, if we permit Him to do so, raise us from and through suffering to His perfect joy. Suffering will be for time alone; eternity will be joy. Nietzsche's aspiration, "All joy wills to be eternal," will be fulfilled for those who choose God. How thankful we should be that God is incapable of suffering. The Cross, tolerable as the way, in fact to holy souls an austere joy, would be intolerable as the end. Those who speak of a cross in the heart of God are unwittingly preaching despair. The problem of suffering can be solved, only if it can be ended. . . .

Though God is, and must be, above suffering, neverthless He has entered into the most intimate union with suffering mankind. For He has entered into personal union with the Soul and Body that in the Passion tasted the utmost of suffering. God has sanctified and redeemed suffering by assuming it to His person, though incapable of sharing it. In the crucified Saviour the Godhead that is beyond suffering, able to raise us beyond it, and suffering humanity meet. The Cross is thus at the centre of the problem of suffering.

EDWARD I. WATKIN
(1888–)

The Crucifixion

"A Paltry Sacrifice."—Preface to a Play

Oh, man's capacity
For spiritual sorrow, corporal pain!
Who has explored the deepmost of that sea,
With heavy links of a far-fathoming chain?

That melancholy lead,
Let down in guilty and in innocent hold,
Yes into childish hands deliverèd,
Leaves the sequestered floor unreached, untold.

One only has explored
The deepmost; but He did not die of it.
Not yet, not yet He died. Man's human Lord
Touched the extreme; it is not infinite.

But over the abyss
Of God's capacity for woe He stayed
One hesitating hour; what gulf was this?
Forsaken He went down, and was afraid.

ALICE MEYNELL
(1847–1922)

At Four Crossing Roads

Cymen: Sacrifice
Can only perfectly be made by God
And sacrifice has so been made, by God
To God in the body of God with man,
On a tree set up at the four crossing roads
Of earth, heaven, time, and eternity
Which meet upon that cross. I have heard this;
And while we listened, with our eyes half-shut
Facing the late sun, above the shoulder
Of the speaking man I saw the cross-road tree,
The love of the God hung on the motes and beams
Of light.[1]

CHRISTOPHER FRY
(1907-   )

Justice and Mercy Have Met

That man should be delivered by Christ's passion was in keeping
with both His mercy and His justice—with His justice, because by
His passion Christ made satisfaction for the sin of the human

---

[1] In *Thor With Angels*, Cymen, with his tribesmen, has just been converted
from Saxon paganism to Christianity by St. Augustine of Kent (596 A.D.).

race, and so man was set free by Christ's justice; and with His
mercy, for since man of himself could not satisfy for the sin of all
human nature . . . God gave him His Son to satisfy for him:
"Being justified freely by His grace, through the redemption that
is in Christ Jesus, whom God hath proposed to be a propitiation,
through faith in His blood" (Rom. iii.24, 25). And this came of
more copious mercy than if He had forgiven sins without satisfaction: "God, who is rich in mercy, for His exceeding charity
wherewith He loved us, even when we were dead in sins, hath
quickened us together in Christ" (Eph. ii.4).

SAINT THOMAS AQUINAS
(1225?–1274)

Balances

 . . . If there be a power too just and strong
To wink at crimes, and bear unpunished wrong;
Look humbly upward, see his will disclose
The forfeit first, and then the fine impose:
A mulct thy property could never pay,
Had not Eternal Wisdom found the way,
And with celestial wealth supplied thy store:
His justice makes the fine, his mercy quits the score.
See God descending in thy human frame;
The offended suffering in the offender's name;
All thy misdeeds to him imputed see,
And all his righteousness devolved on thee.

For granting we have sinned, and that the offence
Of man is made against Omnipotence,
Some price that bears proportion must be paid,
And infinite with infinite be weighed.

JOHN DRYDEN
(1631–1700)

They Know Not What They Do

Even from the Cross, when Our Lord in His agony found the
perfection of His saintly Humanity—even then He did not own
Himself a victim of injustice: *They know not what they do*. Words
that have meaning for the youngest child, words some would like
to call childish, but the spirits of evil must have been muttering
them ever since without understanding, and with ever-growing
terror. Instead of the thunderbolts they awaited, it is as though a
Hand of innocence closed over the chasm of their dwelling.

GEORGES BERNANOS
(1888–1948)

The Word of the Cross

Look on thy God, Christ hidden in our flesh.
A bitter word, the cross, and bitter sight:
Hard rind without, to hold the heart of heaven.
Yet sweet it is, for God upon that tree
Did offer up His life: upon that rood
My life hung, that my life might stand in God.
Christ, what am I to give Thee for my life?
Unless take from Thy hands the cup they hold,

To cleanse me with the precious draught of death.
What shall I do? My body to be burned?
Make myself vile? The debt's not paid out yet.
Whate'er I do, it is but I and Thou,
And still do I come short, still must Thou pay
My debts, O Christ; for debts Thyself hadst none.
What love may balance Thine? My Lord was found
In fashion like a slave, that so His slave
Might find himself in fashion like his Lord.
Think you the bargain's hard, to have exchanged
The transient for the eternal, to have sold
Earth to buy Heaven? More dearly God bought me.

SAINT PAULINUS OF NOLA
(353–431)
Translated from the Latin by
Helen Waddell

IV

IMAGE AND SYMBOL

If Christianity claims to have a truth superior to any other truth in its symbolism, then it is the symbol of the cross in which this is expressed, the cross of Christ.

PAUL TILLICH
(1886–   )

THE SONG TO THE LAMB

And I saw upon the right hand of him who sits upon the throne a scroll written within and without, sealed with seven seals. And I saw a strong angel proclaiming with a loud voice, "Who is worthy to open the scroll, and to break the seals thereof?" And no one in heaven, or on earth or under the earth, was able to open the scroll or to look thereon. And I wept much, because no one was found worthy to open the scroll or to look thereon.

And one of the elders said to me, "Do not weep; behold, the lion of the tribe of Juda, the root of David, has overcome to open the scroll and its seven seals." And I saw, and behold, in the midst of the throne of the four living creatures, and in the midst of the elders, a Lamb standing, as if slain, having seven horns and seven eyes, which are the seven spirits of God sent forth into all the earth. And he came and took the scroll out of the right hand of him who sat upon the throne. And when he had opened the scroll, the four living creatures and the twenty-four elders fell down before the Lamb having each a harp and golden bowls full of incense, which are the prayers of the saints.

And they sing a new canticle, saying,
"Worthy art thou to take the scroll and to open its seals;
For thou wast slain, and hast redeemed us for God with thy blood,
Out of every tribe and tongue and people and nation,
And hast made them for our God a kingdom and priests,
And they shall reign over the earth."

And I beheld, and I heard a voice of many angels round about the throne, and the living creatures and the elders, and the number of them was thousands of thousands, saying with a loud voice,

*"Worthy is the Lamb who was slain to receive power and
    divinity
and wisdom and strength
and honor and glory and blessing."*

*And every creature that is in heaven and on earth and under
the earth, and such as are on the sea, and all that are in them, I
heard them all saying,*

*"To him who sits upon the throne, and to the Lamb,
blessing and honor and glory and dominion,
forever and ever."*

*And the four living creatures said, "Amen," and the elders fell
down and worshipped him who lives forever and ever.*

SAINT JOHN
Apocalypse 5

Of Pictures and Images

Gregory saith, that pictures are not to be put away because they are not to be worshipped: for paintings appear to move the mind more than descriptions: for deeds are placed before the eyes in paintings, and so appear to be actually carrying on. . . .

The image of the Saviour is more commonly represented in churches in three ways: as sitting on His throne, or hanging on His cross, or lying on the bosom of His mother. And because John Baptist pointed to him saying, "Behold the Lamb of God," therefore some represented Christ under the form of a Lamb. But because the light passeth away, and because Christ is very man, therefore, saith Adrian, Pope, He must be represented in the form of a man. A holy lamb must not be depicted on the cross as a principal object: but there is no let when Christ hath been represented as a man, to paint a lamb in a lower or less prominent part of the picture: since He is the True Lamb *which taketh away the sins of the world*. In these and divers other manners is the image of the Saviour painted, on account of diversity of significations.

WILLIAM DURANDUS
(1237?–1296)

The Stumbling-Block

When it was proclaimed of old, this mystery of the cross had to be hidden by the use of images. Had it been proclaimed without them and presented to us naked, it would have been an even greater stumbling-block. And the more superb the mystery, the more it had to remain under the shadow of imagery, so that its very hardness for our understanding should impel us ever anew to seek the grace of God.

TERTULLIAN
(160?–230?)

At the Centre of the World

Already in Jewish prophecy the tree of life with the four-fold stream of water around it[1] was an image representing Messianic salvation.[2] Indeed the divine Wisdom was itself this tree of life[3] and the author of the New Testament Apocalypse sees the fulfilment of redemption under the same image.[4] But here there enters a new element which makes all the difference. "A right to the tree of life"[5] is reserved to those who have washed their robes in the blood of the Lamb. Between the tree of life in Paradise and the tree of life of the New Heaven the ancient Christian saw towering up yet another tree of life on which the fate of the children of Adam is decided—the cross—, and with his mystic's eye he saw these trees all within the framework of a single image. The tree of Paradise is only a prefiguration of the cross and this cross is the centre of the world and of the drama of man's salvation. It towers from Golgotha to heaven, gathering the whole world together, and was set up in the same place where Adam was created, where he lies buried and where at the same hour of the same

---

[1] Gen. ii.9, 10.
[2] Cf. Ezek. xlvii.12; also the Book of Enoch xxiv.3-6; xxv.1-7.
[3] Prov. iii.18.
[4] Apoc. ii.7; xxii.2.
[5] Apoc. xxii.14.

day the second Adam was to die; and at its foot there stream the four rivers of Paradise. These are the rivers of the mystery of baptism by means of which Adam's posterity obtains a new right to the ever green tree of life. A Christian poem of the third century begins with the words:

> *Est locus ex omni medius quem credimus orbe*
> *Golgotha Iudaei patrio cognomine dicunt.*[6]
> (There is a place which we believe to be the centre of the world.
> The Jews give it the native name of Golgotha.)

Then the poet describes how this cross—tree of life—grows to an immense height, how it stretches out its arms, gathering the whole round world in its grasp, how at its foot the baptismal spring bubbles forth and how all nations hurry to the spot to drink everlasting life. The poem closes with the lines:

> *Inde iter ad caelum per ramos arboris altae,*
> *Hoc lignum vitae cunctis credentibus. Amen.*
> (Thence we go to heaven by way of the branches
> of the high tree.
> This is the wood of life to all that believe. Amen.)

HUGO RAHNER
(1900–   )

This Tree Wide as the Heavens

This tree, wide as the heavens itself, has grown up into heaven from the earth. It is an immortal growth and towers twixt heaven and earth. It is the fulcrum of all things and the place where they

---

[6] Pseudo-Cyprian, *Carmen de Pascha vel de Ligno Vitae.*

are at rest. It is the foundation of the round world, the centre of the cosmos. In it all the diversities in our human nature are formed into a unity. It is held together by invisible nails of the Spirit so that it may not break loose from the divine. It touches the highest summits of heaven and makes the earth firm beneath its foot, and it grasps the middle regions between them with its immeasurable arms. . . .

O crucified One, thou leader of the mystical dances! O this spiritual wedding feast! O this divine Pasch that passes from heaven to earth and rises up again to heaven! O this new feast of all things! O cosmic festal gathering! O joy of the universe, honour, ecstasy, exquisite delight by which dark death is destroyed, life returns to all and the gates of heaven are opened. God appeared as a man and man rose up as God when he shattered the gates of Hell and burst the iron bolts thereof. And the people that were in the depths arise from the dead and announce to all the hosts of heaven: "The thronging choir from earth is coming home."

SAINT HIPPOLYTUS OF ROME

(early 3rd century)

Constantine's Vision

According to legend, the pagan Emperor Constantine, son of Saint Helena, was assured one night of victory in battle by an apparition of the Cross of his mother's faith shining in the heavens. Around it appeared the words, "In this sign thou shalt conquer." In the *Elene*, the Old English version by Cynewulf, the Emperor is converted and sends his mother to Jerusalem to find where the true Cross, symbolized in his vision, has been concealed since the death of

Christ. She finds it buried on Calvary where she has
been led by a Jew named Judas. Constantine commands her to build a church on Calvary to enshrine
the Cross which she has covered with gold and jewels.

> "There from that time   the Tree of life
> Best Tree of triumph   has had its abode
> In beauty unbroken."

The following selection from the *Elene* describes
Constantine's vision:

Then to great Caesar   as he lay in slumber
Asleep with his train   was a vision revealed.
To him appeared   a beauteous Presence,
In man's shape   made manifest,
White and shining,   more fair of form
Than early or late   he beheld under heaven.
He started from slumber,   did on his boar-helm,
And straightway the herald,   fair heavenly form,
Spoke unto Caesar,   named him by name
And the veil of darkness   vanished away:
    "O Constantine,   the King of angels,
Leader of nations   and Lord of fate,
Proclaims a compact.   Be not afraid
Though these foreign tribes   threaten with terror,
With hard battle.   To heaven look up,
To the Prince of glory.   There find support
And a token of triumph."

                     Straightway the king
Opened his heart   to the angel's bidding
And looked on high   as the herald bade,
Fair weaver of concord.   Clothed with treasure
O'er the roof of clouds   he beheld the Cross
Adorned with gold;   its jewels glittered.
The radiant Tree   was written round
With gleaming letters   of glowing light:

"With this sign thou shalt halt   the hostile host,
And crush the foe   in this perilous fray."
   Then the radiance faded   faring on high,
And the angel with it,   to the host of the holy.

CYNEWULF
(died 785)
Translated from the Old English by
Charles W. Kennedy

The Sum of Nature

Society [under Constantine] was almost wholly pagan in its point of view, and was drawn to the Cross because, in its system of physics, the Cross had absorbed all the old occult or fetish-power. The symbol represented the sum of nature—the Energy of modern science—and society believed it to be as real as X-rays; perhaps it was! The emperors used it like gunpowder in politics; the physicians used it like rays in medicine; the dying clung to it as the quintessence of force, to protect them from the forces of evil on their road to the next life.

HENRY ADAMS
(1838–1918)

The Exaltation of the Holy Cross

We may note that before the Passion of Christ, the tree of the cross was a tree of paltry price, because crosses were made of cheap wood. It was a tree of unfruitfulness, because in whatever numbers it was planted on the hill of Calvary, it bore no fruit. It was a tree of shame, because it was used for the execution of criminals. It was a tree of darkness, because it was dark and without beauty. It was a tree of death, because men were put to death upon it. It was a tree of evil smell, because it was planted in the midst of rotting corpses. But after the Passion it was many-wise exalted. Its paltriness was changed into preciousness, whence Andrew said: "Hail, cross of great price!" Its barrenness was changed into fruitfulness, whence it is written in the *Canticles*: "I will go up into the palm tree, and will take hold of the fruit thereof!" Its shame was changed into sublime nobility, as Augustine says: "The cross, which was the gibbet of criminals, has passed over to the foreheads of emperors." Its darkness turned into light, as Chrysostom says: "On the day of judgement, the Cross and the wounds of Christ will be more lucent than the rays of the sun." Its death passed into everlasting life, whence we sing: "Whence death arose, thence life might rise again." Its evil smell became the odour of sweetness, whence we read in the *Canticles*: "While the king was at his repose, my spikenard (which is to say, the Holy Cross) sent forth the odour thereof."

JACOBUS DE VORAGINE
(1230?–1298)

The King's Tree

Medieval legend relates that a seed of cedar, cypress, and pine taken from the tree whose fruit Adam had eaten were placed by his son Seth under Adam's tongue when he died. Seth had found the tree in Paradise, first with a serpent twisted about it, then with an infant in its highest branches. The infant was Christ who was to bring to Adam's progeny the oil of mercy. The seeds respectively symbolized the Father, the Son, and the Holy Spirit. They finally grew into a single trunk which ultimately became the wood of the cross of Christ. From the beginning, the separate wands worked marvels. Moses transplanted them, sweetened the bitter desert waters with them, and smote the rock. David caused them to become one tree under which he composed the Psalms. Solomon had the tree felled to form the master-beam for the temple, but it was always either too long or too short. When the Queen of Sheba visited Solomon, the tree was used as a bridge over the brook of Cedron, but she waded in the water rather than dishonor it. Taking up the story at the time of Christ's passion, the legend says:

When Christ a thousand years [after the death of Solomon], betrayed by Judas was about to suffer death, the Jews would have none but the King's Tree whereon to hang him. They went, therefore, to the temple and hewed it into the shape of the Cross; but not a foot could they raise it or stir it from its place. But when Jesus was brought, he louted down and kissed it, and without help of man he laid it upon his back. This was the Holy Rood on which he died. And after he had given up the ghost, that Rood blossomed from the hour of noon even unto the going down of the sun.

CHARLES MILLS GAYLEY[1]
(1858–1932)

The Making of the Cross

Rough fir, hauled from the hills. And the tree it had been,
Lithe-limbed, wherein the wren had nested,

[1] Gayley's version in *Plays of Our Forefathers* is a composite of the anonymous account in the rhymed *Cursor Mundi* (c.1300) and the prose account by Jacobus de Voragine (died 1298?). The summary given above is by the editor.

Whereon the red hawk and the grey
Rested from flight, and the raw-head vulture
Shouldered to his feed—that tree went over
Bladed down with a double-bitted axe; was snaked with winches;
The wedge split it; hewn with the adze
It lay to season toward its use.

So too with the nails: milleniums under the earth,
Pure ore; chunked out with picks; the nail-shape
Struck in the pelt-lunged forge; tonged to a cask
And the wait against that work.

Even the thorn-bush flourished from afar,
As do the flourishing generations of its kind,
Filling the shallow soil no one wants;
Wind-sown, it cuts the cattle and the wild horse;
It tears the cloth of man, and hurts his hand.

Just as in life the good things of the earth
Are patiently assembled: some from here, some from there;
Wine from the hill and wheat from the valley;
Rain that comes blue-bellied out of the sopping sea;
Snow that keeps its drift on the gooseberry ridge,
Will melt with May, go down, take the egg of the salmon,
Serve the traffic of otters and fishes,
Be ditched to orchards . . .

So too are gathered up all the possibles of evil.

And when the Cross was joined, quartered,
As is the earth; spoked, as is the Universal Wheel—
Those radials that led all unregenerate act
Inward to innocence—it met the thorn-wove Crown;

It found the Scourges and the Dice;
The Nail was given and the reed-lifted Sponge;
The Curse caught forward out of the heart corrupt;
The excoriate Foul, stoned with the thunder and the hail—
All these made up that miscellaneous wrath
And were assumed.

The evil and the wastage and the woe,
As if the earth's old cyst, back down the slough
To Adam's sin-burnt calcinated bones
Rushed out of time and clotted on the Cross.

Off there the cougar
Coughed in passion when the sun went out; the rattler
Filmed his glinty eye, and found his hole.

BROTHER ANTONINUS
(1912–   )

The New Jacob's Ladder

The Cross of Christ is the Jacob's ladder by which we ascend into
the highest heavens. There we see joyful patriarchs, expecting
saints, prophets ministering, apostles publishing, and doctors
teaching, all nations concentering, and angels praising. That
Cross is a tree set on fire with invisible flame, that illuminateth
all the world. The flame is love: the love in His bosom who died
on it, in the light of which we see how to possess all the things
in heaven and earth after His similitude. For He that suffered on
it was the Son of God as you are: though He seemed only a mortal
man. He had acquaintance and relations as you have, but He

was a lover of men and angels. Was he not the Son of God; and heir of the whole world? To this poor, bleeding, naked Man did all the corn and wine, and oil, and gold and silver in the world minister in an invisible manner, even as He was exposed lying and dying upon the Cross.

THOMAS TRAHERNE
(1637?–1674)

Pilgrim's Progress

Now I saw in my dream, that the highway up which Christian was to go, was fenced on either side with a wall, and that wall was called Salvation. Up this way, therefore, did burdened Christian run, but not without great difficulty, because of the load on his back.

He ran thus till he came at a place somewhat ascending, and upon that place stood a cross, and a little below, in the bottom, a sepulchre. So I saw in my dream, that just as Christian came up with the cross, his burden loosed from off his shoulders, and fell from off his back, and began to tumble, and so continued to do, till it came to the mouth of the sepulchre, where it fell in, and I saw it no more.

Then was Christian glad and lightsome, and said, with a merry heart, "He hath given me rest by His sorrow, and life by His death." Then he stood still awhile to look and wonder; for it was very surprising to him, that the sight of the cross should thus ease him of his burden. He looked, therefore, and looked again, even till the springs that were in his head sent the waters down his cheeks. Now, as he stood looking and weeping, behold, three Shining Ones came to him and saluted him with "Peace be to thee." So the first said to him, "Thy sins be forgiven thee." The second stripped him of his rags, and clothed him with change of raiment. The third also set a mark in his forehead, and gave him a roll with a seal upon it, which he bid him look on as he ran, and that he should give it in at the Celestial Gate. So they went their way.

JOHN BUNYAN
(1628–1688)

Two Théorèmes Spirituels

I

Great Sun, flame of Christ,
You have passed through four houses of the Zodiac:
Through Virgo, where Christ was born of flesh
From His soul, matched and matchless;
Through the Waterbearer, when He sorrowed
In tears, blameless; through the Bull,
When He offered His body on the gallows.
Now he enters the house of the Lion
With a mane of light whose beams
Enflame the hemispheres, and His voice
Is the shaking thunder, the roar from the grave
That brings the world of beasts to the yoke
Of His redemption.

II

O Phoenix, cherished bird of Arabia,
You are the symbol of Christ the Hero.
He, like you, lies unenslaved among the dead.

You die on a scented pyre;
He dies on a tree that offers heaven its perfume.
Your ashes are his marrow;
You bear your ashes to an altar in the burning desert.
Christ, so resurrected, against the azure sky
And the vaults of stars You raise your tree of light.

JEAN DE LA CEPPÈDE

(1550–1622)

Translated from the French by
Clinton Larson

Bull

From The Christ of Velázquez, Part One, XXIII

                    White Bull with a crescent moon on
                        Your forehead,

Leviticus 4. 3   young Bullock without blemish, who bent
                    to the yoke from the cross,
                    sprinkling Your blood on the earth,
                    the altar of Your Father's temple;

Leviticus 16. 6   Calf of expiation, flock's
                    bellwether, priest as well as

Hebrews 7. 27   victim offering Yourself;

Leviticus 11. 3–4   we can eat of You, who pasture on our sad
                        sorrow
                    and with cloven feet furrow our valleys—
                    verdure watered by our tears—
                    for Your flesh is clean.
                    Calf of flesh sustained
                    with the harvest of work the sons

Exodus 32. 4–20

of Adam reaped in their sweat, You burn
the golden calf in Your fire, reduce it
to powder, strew it upon the water
and make us drink of it, and thus gain
pardon for us from Your Father!

MIGUEL DE UNAMUNO
(1864–1936)
Translated from the Spanish by
Anthony Kerrigan

The Passion as Poetic Tragedy

I had said of Christ that he ranks with the poets. That is true.
But his entire life also is the most wonderful of poems. For "pity
and terror" there is nothing in the entire cycle of Greek tragedy
to touch it. The absolute purity of the protagonist . . . shows how
wrong Aristotle was when he said in his treatise on the drama
that it would be impossible to bear the spectacle of one blameless
in pain. Nor in Aeschylus nor Dante, those stern masters of tenderness, in Shakespeare, the most purely human of all the great
artists, in the whole of Celtic myth and legend, where the love-
liness of the world is shown through a mist of tears, and the life
of a man is no more than the life of a flower, is there anything
that, for sheer simplicity of pathos wedded and made one with
sublimity of tragic effect, can be said to equal or even approach
the last act of Christ's passion. The little supper with his companions, one of whom has already sold him for a price; the anguish
in the quiet moon-lit garden; the false friend coming close to him
so as to betray him with a kiss; the friend who still believed in
him, and on whom as on a rock he had hoped to build a house of
refuge for Man, denying him as the bird cried to the dawn; his

own utter loneliness, his submission, his acceptance of everything; and along with it all such scenes as the high priest of orthodoxy rending his raiment in wrath and the magistrate of civil justice calling for water in the vain hope of cleansing himself of that stain of innocent blood that makes him the scarlet figure of history; the coronation ceremony of sorrow, one of the most wonderful things in the whole of recorded time; the crucifixion of the Innocent One before the eyes of his mother and of the disciple whom he loved; the soldiers gambling and throwing dice for his clothes; the terrible death by which he gave the world its most eternal symbol; and his final burial in the tomb of the rich man, his body swathed in Egyptian linen with costly spices and perfumes as though he had been a king's son. When one contemplates all this from the point of view of art alone, one cannot but be grateful that the supreme office of the Church should be the playing of the tragedy without the shedding of blood: the mystical presentation, by means of dialogue and costume and gesture even, of the Passion of her Lord; and it is always a source of pleasure and awe to me to remember that the ultimate survival of the Greek chorus, lost elsewhere to art, is to be found in the servitor answering the priest at Mass.

OSCAR WILDE
(1854–1900)

Madrigal

A lo divino:
of Christ and the soul

Once a young shepherd went off to despond:
how could he dance again? how could he sing?

All of his thoughts to his shepherdess cling,
with love in his heart a ruinous wound.

The root of his sorrow? No, never the wound:
the lad was a lover and welcomed the dart
that lodged where it drank the red race of his heart—
but spurned by his fairest, went off to despond.

For only to think he was spurned, and by one
radiant shepherdess, drove him afar;
cost him a drubbing in foreigners' war,
with love in his heart like a ruinous wound.

The shepherd boy murmured: O murrain descend
on the traitor estranging my angel and me!
charming her vision that stares stonily
on the love in my heart like a ruinous wound.

Time passed: on a season he sprang from the ground,
swarmed a tall tree and arms balancing wide
beautifully grappled the tree till he died
of the love in his heart like a ruinous wound,

SAINT JOHN OF THE CROSS
(1542–1591)
Translated from the Spanish by
John Frederick Nims

The Nightingale

I want to go a-maying
    In Jesus' passion brave.
There be for aye my staying
    In life beyond the grave.

It is a flowery bower
    Bedewed with many a tear.
My grief would die the hour
    That I might enter there.

One hears the nightingale chanting
    Under the stinging thorn.
His heart is of love descanting,
    Who wants can hear him mourn.

From the thornbush in the garden
    The nightingale sings his adieu:
"Father, grant them pardon.
    They know not what they do."

The murderer was fawning
    For mercy, his coveted prize.
The nightingale sang, "Ere morning
    Thou shalt be in Paradise."

"Oh, John, behold thy mother.
    Oh, mother, behold thy Son.
I bind you to each other.
    Be thou her guardian, John."

"My God," his voice was bursting,
    "My God, why leavest Thou me?"
His heart within was thirsting.
    To drink desired he.

What was it he was drinking?
    Vinegar mixed with gall.
His tired head was sinking,
    He sang, "Fulfilled is all."

"Into Thy hands my spirit,
    Oh Father, I commend."
And with that gentle lyric
    To another forest he went.

He let the tender violet
    Stand at the cross's base,
Who formerly in Nazareth
    Received him with humble grace.

The open rose he bade it
    Hang on the cross above,
Its petals fell and faded:
    The nightingale died of love.

ANONYMOUS
(1300–1500)
Netherlands; translated by
Adriaan J. Barnouw

A Spiritual Song

A bed of billowing flowers is painting symbols,
Tracing exotic embroideries.
God's blue breath
Blows into the arbor, gaily.
A cross stands high
In the wild grapevines.

I hear many, oh many
Who celebrate close by in the village.
A gardener is mowing near the wall;
Softly an organ is pealing,
Blending music and golden light.
Love blesses the Bread and Wine.

Girls, too, are coming in,
And at last a cock is crowing.
Gently a broken-down gate is opened,
And there, amid the wreaths,
Among rows of roses, rows of roses,
Rests Mary, fragile and fair.[1]

The beggar there at the old rock
Is as still as if dead in his prayer.
Tenderly a shepherd from the hill
And an angel sing in the glade—
Nearby in the glade,—and the song is borne
To the ears of sleeping children.

GEORG TRAKL
(1887–1914)
Translated from the German by
Frida Grosser

The Sign Made of Charity

We begin the divine Liturgy by signing ourselves with the Cross in
the name of the Father and the Son and the Holy Spirit. We trace
on ourselves the form of the Cross whose mystery we are about to
live. We call upon the everlasting Love of which, at the cross-

---

[1] The lines suggest the term *Maria im Rosenhag* applied to pictures of Our
Lady in a floral setting or rose arbor.

roads of history, the Cross is the bleeding ecstasy. We invoke the indivisible Trinity to whom this sacrifice is offered by the Sacred Humanity which subsists in the Word.

We adore the Father who expresses Himself by uttering the Word, the Word who affirms Himself by expressing the Father, and the Spirit who wills Himself as the eternal flame of the kiss that unites them. We confess the mysterious fecundity of the Supreme Unity, and the infinite holiness of the relations in which the Persons consist. For here is hidden the mystery of unfathomable charity: the Divine Life does not subsist, does not issue into a personal centre, save as an outgoing towards another, and the Self of each Person is wholly ecstasy and wholly altruism; the incommunicability of the self is based upon an eternal communication, the appropriation of being is its absolute and complete gift, no selfishness is conceivable, no return upon self, no self-satisfaction and no "possession"! The eternal purity of boundless Love discloses in the treasure of its abysses a glimpse of Poverty's holiest and most sublime Countenance.

Faith . . . beholds the mystery of eternal Holiness in the infinite altruism of an everlasting charity. This surely is suggested by St. John's words in his first Epistle. "We know and believe the love that God hath to us. God *is* love."

Can we then be surprised that the expression in time of the Divine Life—in the Incarnation of the Word—was completed on the Cross in the anathema of the most cruel poverty—and in the infinite opening of the outstretched arms?

Deep calls to deep in their incomprehensible interchanges, each a reciprocal and unfathomable *de profundis*. . . .

In the name of the Father, and of the Son, and of the Holy Spirit. Amen.

MAURICE ZUNDEL
(contemporary)

Confession

From my poor sins I am set free.
In lilac dusk the taper smolders;
The dark stole's rigid drapery
Conceals a massive head and shoulders.

"Talitha kumi":[1] Is it He
Once more? How fast the heart is beating . . .
A touch: a hand moves absently
The customary cross repeating.

ANNA AKHMATOVA
(1893–　　)
Translated from the Russian by
Babette Deutsch and Avraham Yarmolinsky

Saeta[1]

The dark Christ
changes
from the lily of Judea
to the carnation of Spain.
　Look　there　where　He　comes!

Of Spain!—
Sky limpid, somber,
The earth baked,

---

[1] "Girl, arise!" Uttered by Christ when He restored the dead girl to life.
[2] Untranslatable. Literally, an arrow of prayer shot from the heart to a holy image during processions in Holy Week.

And ditches with water flowing
Most slowly.

The dark Christ
of the burnt locks,
the staring cheek bones,
with eyes lost in their whites.
Look there where He goes!

FEDERICO GARCÍA LORCA
(1899–1936)
*Translated from the Spanish by
Sister M. Katharine Elaine, C.S.C.*

Passion in the Andes

Some few years ago I went on a spring cruise. The steamer touched
the northern tip of South America and paused for a day at the port
so that passengers might travel up the mountain to Caracas. When
we reached Venezuela word came that Gomez, the old dictator,
lay dying in the capital. And as we went up the winding road, . . .
I noticed that all those who walked along the highway were clad
in black or purple. Young and old all seemed to be hurrying to
some central point. And, naturally, it was my notion that they were
hurrying to the palace to learn the fate of Gomez. . . .

But at the door of the cathedral the driver stopped and said
something to my companion. My friend translated and explained,
"The driver says this is the service to mark the three hours of
agony on the cross."

And it came to me that they mourned not for Gomez but for
the Son of God. Out of bright sunlight I came into cool darkness

flecked, but not wholly broken, by the light of many hundred candles. And all about the walls and statues and across the shoulders of the worshipers I saw the badge of purple. Holy Week had come to the foothills of the Andes.

I have seen church services in far and near places, and many were impressive, but here for the first time I saw a people who seemed to feel that the Passion of the Lord was actually occurring once again.

Pilate was not a famous dead procurator of Judea who washed his hands in an ancient city long ago. It was but yesterday that Jesus stood before the Romans on trial for His life and was condemned. And at the very moment the living Christ hung on the cross.

An Indian woman, older than any being I had ever seen before, lifted her head from the floor as she prayed that death should not achieve its victory. Children in their purple smocks looked at the dancing lights and wondered. But they were silent.

It was as if someone of their own lay dying in a room at home. And all of them lived in a world in which each year Jesus again walked the earth and Judas brought betrayal in a pleasant garden. Many stood outside upon the steps under the hot sun and peered through the doors and down the dark aisles. They waited for some word from the mourners. Almost they seemed to say, "What is the news? How fares our Lord on Calvary?"

The faith of the faithful burns high along that mountain shelf. Some part of the agony is theirs, but the joy of resurrection bursts in their heart like an apple tree suddenly come to bloom. To them the miracle is without question. They have lived through it, and rebirth becomes a part of their own experience.

HEYWOOD BROUN
(1888–1939)

Nocturne of the Descent

Christ of the countryside, Christ of the hilltop shrine,
I came to beg your healing for my sick flesh,
but now that I see you, my eyes move
from your body to my own, ashamed.
My blood is still a flowing stream;
Yours is quick no longer; it is stopped like water in a dam.
I have a shoulder to lean upon;
yet even the four nails no longer support you,
and my meeting with you becomes a gathering up of your blood,
that blood that is like an answering tongue.
Our coming together becomes a passing of my hands over my
    shrunken breast,
a catching hold of your feet, like two fish dripping.

And I remember nothing any longer—
not the journey, nor the weariness, nor the pain.
The urgency of the plea I was bringing you
dies on my beggar's lips
as I find myself, this wretched nightfall,
on a slope before a conquered hulk
which falls and falls and falls forever
in a way no one had told me.
From your high vertical there, your flesh falls still
like skin ripped from fruit;
your breast falls, your knees,
and, like a broken bud, your head.

Oh, keep falling, Christ—fall into my arms,
O divine burden, O burden of sorrow delivered unto me,

for I am alone in this slanting light,
and what I see may not be seen by any other.
All I see may perhaps happen every night
with no one to understand it, or even know it.
And this fall—since they do not see it,
they do not break it, those who call themselves your children.
They are not guilty of your blood,
for the height is solitude itself,
and the light is so scanty, and so oblique
on a nameless hill rising from the earth.

GABRIELA MISTRAL
(1889–1957)
Translated from the Spanish by
Sister M. Katharine Elaine, C.S.C.

The Wooden Christ

In his father's home, a farmer who's a hundred
Carves a wooden model Lord that works some wonders.

On the face of Jesus he inscribes his misery
When they sent his son to prison in Siberia.

He cuts deep, the wood dust drops, the god doll gazes—
Anguished god indeed, created by its maker.

He, to crucify himself his heart and torments,
Spears the side of God and spikes the palms and insteps.

Then he twists a crown of thorns to grave the forehead;
White the wood the old man gouges, goads and tortures.

With the hands at rest upon the knobby kneecaps,
Wooden Christ himself is born, alive, and painwracked.

Chips pile up to ease the heart, for Christ is risen,
Christ himself is risen from the old man's chisel.

Now the godwright glows, and now he sees the miracle:
Round the head of Christ are lightrays in a circle.

When he stripped the final splinter from the icon,
You could hear the lips of the creator speaking:

"God, I don't believe this piece of wood requires
Labor out of me to bring about a miracle.

"God, you wipe my tears dry, turn my pain to sweetness
Through your agony with both your temples bleeding.

"If you do perform them—miracles, I beg you:
Save the innocent, but punish persecutors!"

And, when he had borne the statue, why
All the people of the land returned to virtue.

And, his lips against the wound of Jesus' passion,
He himself begged mercy for his youth's transgressions.

FAUSTAS KIRŠA
(1891–   )
*Translated from the Lithuanian by
Theodore Melnechuk*

Not Without Bread

Man did not live by bread alone—but he could not live without it. The old monks had the same idea. They planted the Cross in the middle of a desert—and then planted corn and fruit trees, so that the barren symbol flowered into a green reality. They knew, better than most, that man was a creature of flesh and spirit, but that the spirit could not function except in and through the flesh. When the body was sick, the moral responsibility of man was reduced. Man was a thinking reed, but the reed must be anchored firmly in black earth, watered at the roots, warmed by the sun.

MORRIS L. WEST
(1916-   )

Image and Reality

A crucifix is not a picture of Christ on the cross; it *is* Christ on the cross—Christ himself in wood or stone, as Christ himself would be if he were *made* of wood or stone,—a wooden Christ or a stone Christ, not an imitation in wood or stone of Christ made of flesh and blood.

ERIC GILL
(1882–1940)

The Christ of the Fields

Outside, around the chapel, lies the peace of the fields.
And at the dusty crossroads, among the oats,
amid chicory and agrimony,

stands a great Christ of hollow wood where the bees
make their nest. And one can see them in the sunlight,
busy, filled with honey. Coming and going,
they are like black letters written on the sky.

What food would you give to your God, if not honey?

Sometimes the road-mender breaking stones
lifts his head and sees the Christ, the only
friend he has on this road where noon beats down.
To break the stones he goes on his knees
in the shadow of this Christ whose side is crimson.
Then all the honey sings in the sun.

The poet contemplates and ponders. He tells himself
before the slow-waving fields, that each ear
is a wise colony of God's people,
an ear whose every grain longs to be vivified
with water from the grottoes of heaven.
He tells himself that hereafter this grain will grow
in the precious azure which everything makes more blue.
Again he says that in the image of the Son of God,
born also in a grotto, this wheat will feed the hungry.
And the ear born in its turn of the blade
will be shaped like a spire at dawn.

FRANCIS JAMMES
(1868–1938)
Translated from the French by
Sister Mary Immaculate, C.S.C.

Paradox

As we have taken the circle as the symbol of reason and madness, we may very well take the cross as the symbol at once of mystery and of health. Buddhism is centripetal, but Christianity is centrifugal: it breaks out. For the circle is perfect and infinite in its nature; but it is fixed for ever in its size; it can never be larger or smaller. But the cross, though it has at its heart a collision and a contradiction, can extend its four arms for ever without altering its shape. Because it has a paradox in its centre it can grow without changing. The circle returns upon itself and is bound. The cross opens its arms to the four winds; it is a signpost for free travelers.

GILBERT K. CHESTERTON
(1874–1936)

For Lifetime and Death

As [the dying Pope John XXIII] gazed at the crucifix on the wall of his bedroom he said, "I have always had Jesus crucified before me, with His arms open to receive all people. . . . This is the task of . . . the Church: to work toward the fulfillment of the prayer of the Divine Master, 'That they may be one, that they may be one.' "

POPE JOHN XXIII
(1881–1963)
From L'Osservatore Romano

The Image on Veronica's Handkerchief

An imperishable handkerchief wiped that majestic face, his very face, his real face, his man's face with a white handkerchief that perishable face; his pitiful face; and to see him then, in that state, the saviour of the human race, to see him thus, him, the saviour of all the human race, what unfeeling heart would not have softened, what eyes, what human eyes would not have shed tears; that face in a perspiration, all covered with sweat, and filth, and dust, all covered with the dust of the roads, all covered with the dust of the soil; the dust of his face, the common dust, everybody's dust, the dust on his face; stuck to it with sweat.

CHARLES PÉGUY
(1873–1914)
Translated from the French by
Julian Green

Jesus! Thy Crucifix

Jesus! thy Crucifix
Enable thee to guess
The smaller size!

Jesus! thy second face
Mind thee in Paradise
Of ours!

EMILY DICKINSON
(1830–1886)

When I Survey the Wondrous Cross

When I survey the wondrous cross
   On which the Prince of Glory died,
My richest gain I count but loss
   And pour contempt on all my pride.

See, from his head, his hands, his feet
   Sorrow and love flow mingled down;
Did e'er such love and sorrow meet
   Or thorns compose so rich a crown?

His dying crimson, like a robe,
   Spreads o'er his body on the tree;
Then am I dead to all the globe,
   And all the globe is dead to me.

Were the whole realm of nature mine,
   That were a present far too small;
Love so amazing, so divine,
   Demands my soul, my life, my all.

ISAAC WATTS
(1674–1748)

The World's Last Night

What if this present were the world's last night?
Mark in thy heart, O Soul, where thou dost dwell,
The picture of Christ crucified, and tell

Whether that countenance can thee affright;
Tears in his eyes quench the amazing light,
Blood fills his frowns, which from his pierced head fell.
And can that tongue adjudge thee unto hell,
Which prayed forgiveness for his foes' fierce spite?
No, no; but as in my idolatry
I said to all my profane mistresses,
"Beauty, of pity, foulness only is
A sign of rigor," so I say to thee,
"To wicked spirits are horrid shapes assigned,
This beauteous form assures a piteous mind."

JOHN DONNE
(1573–1631)

The Crucifix

You whom I have contemplated resting on her lips
As she breathed her last and said her last adieu,
Symbol twice holy, gift of a dying hand
And image of my God,

What tears have flowed on those feet I adore
Since that sacred hour when, from a martyr's breast
To my trembling hands you passed, warm still
From her expiring sigh.

The blessed candles flared in final flame;
The priest murmured those sweet chants of death
Like the plaintive strains a mother sings
To her sleeping child.

Her forehead kept the trace of childlike hope,
And on that face, stricken by immortal beauty,
Fleeting sorrow had imprinted grace
And death its majesty.

The wind that fingered once her unbound hair
Would reveal, then hide again her face from me,
Like the play of shadows on a white cenotaph, shadows
From black cypress trees.

One arm hung down from that bed of death;
Her hand, folded lifelessly above her heart,
Seemed to seek again and press upon her mouth
The image of the Saviour.

When her lips seemed reaching out again to caress it,
Her soul had fled even then into God's embrace,
Like a light fragrance which the flame devours
Before consuming it.

All was in repose now around her icy mouth,
Her breath was stilled,
And over her sightless eyes the fluttering lids
Fell back half closed.

Then I, watching yet, and seized by a secret terror,
Dared not draw near her holy body,
As though death's mute grandeurs
Had consecrated it anew.

I did not dare . . . but the priest heard my silence,
And taking the crucifix from her cold fingers said,

"Here is a remembrance; here is hope.
Take it, my son."

Yes, you will stay with me, O token of her death!
Countless times the tree that I planted
Over her nameless tomb has changed foliage,
But you have never left me.

Placed near this heart, where, alas, all is effaced,
You have defended her against time's oblivion,
And my eyes, drop by drop, have left marks
Upon your softened ivory.

O last confidant of that soul which has taken flight,
Come lie here upon my heart! Speak again and tell me
Those things she said to you when her failing words
Could reach only you.

At that hour of doubt when the soul draws within,
Hides itself beneath the thick veil over our eyes;
And slowly, little by little recedes, freed now from the glassy
    senses,
Deaf to all farewells;

And then, as between life and uncertain death,
Like fruit falling by its weight from its branch,
It hangs and trembles at each breath,
Suspended on the night of the tomb;

When the chants, the mixed harmony of weeping
Can no longer rouse the sleeping spirit
Clinging in its agony to the lips of the dying
As to a last friend:

Then, to illumine the horror of that narrow passage,
To raise again toward God the weakened gaze,
Heavenly Consoler, whose image we kiss,
Tell me, what do you say?

You know, you know how to die, and on that terrible night
When you prayed in vain, the tears of God
Bathed the roots of the sacred olive tree
From evening till morn.

From the cross, where your eyes penetrated that great mystery,
You saw your mother in tears and all nature in mourning,
You left, as we do, your friends on earth,
And your body in the tomb.

In the name of that death by which my weakness deserves
To return to you by a sorrowful sigh,
When my hour shall come, remember your own,
You who know how to die.

I shall seek then the place where her tremulous mouth
Breathed out on your feet the irrevocable adieu,
And her soul will come to guide errant mine
To the heart of that same God.

O grant, grant that on my deathbed,
Both sad and calm, I might, like some desolate angel
With mourning face, be able to embrace with my lips
This sacred heritage.

Sustain my last steps, soothe my last hour,
And be the dedicated pledge of hope and love

Of one who departs to one who remains,
A pledge passing in turn from the dying to the living,

Until the day when, from the dead, piercing the somber vault,
A voice in the heavens, calling them seven times,
Will rouse those who sleep in the shadow
Of the eternal cross.

ALPHONSE DE LAMARTINE
(1790–1869)
Translated from the French by
Sister M. Margaret Denyse, C.S.C.

The Crucifix

When the last great and solemn act was played
And God in torment on the cross was laid,
Then at the foot of the life-giving rood
Mary the sinner and Mary the Virgin stood,
Two women side by side,
Drowned in their grief's immeasurable tide.

But here beneath the cross we contemplate,
As though on duty at the Governor's gate,
Instead of those two holy women, lo,
Two sentries grim, with musket and shako.
Now tell me, Why? This crucifix, maybe,
You guard in state as Government property?
Or thieves, or mice, you fancy, might lay siege?
Or to the King of Kings you'ld add prestige?
Or do you hope by patronage to save
The Lord who is crowned with thorns, the Lord who gave

In willingness His mortal flesh to bear
The Roman torturer's lash, the nails, the spear?
Or else you fear the mob may bring disgrace
On Him who dying saved all Adam's race?
Or, lest his presence irk the modish crowd,
The common man, perhaps, is Not Allowed?

ALEXANDER PUSHKIN
(1799–1837)
Translated from the Russian by
Frances Cornford and E. P. Salaman

The Cross of St. Brigid

Brigid's emblem in Ireland today is a cross woven of rushes, or
straw, and the custom still persists in many districts of weaving
these crosses on the eve of her feast-day and hanging them inside
the eaves of the houses to invoke her blessing on the homes and
land. The emblem and the custom take their origin in the story of
how she once brought about the conversion of a pagan chieftain,
who lived in the neighborhood of Kildare. This man was dying
and some Christian in his household sent for Brigid. When she
arrived, the chieftain was raving. . . . Brigid sat down at his bed-
side and began by consoling him. As was customary in that age,
the floor was strewn with rushes both for warmth and cleanliness.
It was a floor covering easily renewed. Brigid reflectively stooped
down and picked a bunch of rushes from the floor at her feet; she
started to weave them into a cross by fastening the points together.
The sick man asked her what she was doing. She began to explain
the Cross, and as she talked his delirium quietened down and he
questioned her with growing interest. He believed and was bap-
tized at the point of death. That is the reason why the primitive

cross of rushes has been venerated in Ireland for fifteen hundred years. Moreover, the Irish carry this custom around the world with them. I saw the rush cross behind the door of a Boston apartment last year.

ALICE CURTAYNE
(contemporary)

Made in Cruciform

Everything reminds us of the cross. We ourselves are made in the form of a cross. Balm and sweetness exhale from the cross. The unction which overflows from the cross inundates our souls in proportion as we unite ourselves with it, holding it tightly against our hearts. The cross contains more wisdom than any book; all who do not know this book are ignorant, however many other books they may have studied. Those only are truly wise who love and consult this book, who study it deeply. Bitter as this book is, they are never happier than when they can immerse themselves in its bitterness. The more they frequent this school, the more they desire to remain there; never do their studies weary them.

SAINT JEAN MARIE VIANNEY, CURÉ OF ARS
(1786–1859)

Lenten Flowers

Grow in the kingdom of the cross
Primrose, anemone, bluebell, moss

And the ash-tree's purple bud
Dresses the spear that sheds his blood.

With the thorns that pierce his brow
Soft encircling petals grow

For in each flower the secret lies
Of the tree that crucifies.

Garden by the water clear
All must die that enter here!

KATHLEEN RAINE
(1908–   )

From Canticle of Darkness

Stand gentle in my words. It was
The Friday of roses. And there was a rose
Singing the red song of your blossom.
When I came to the rose, there was
Gethsemane. When I came to Gethsemane
There was the rose. Stand gentle in my words.
It was the Friday of Golgotha, the place
Of skull. O cross of petals—
O crossed petals—
Stand gentle in my words. For I thought
It was the rose of crucifixion, till I knew
It was the rose of resurrection. Stand
Gentle in my words. Saying I saw

The things of the world drop their skins.
Saying I saw white wings swanning in
Endless flocks of white. Saying I saw
The earth like a white lamb walking
Beside the mother ewe. Saying I heard
The nations like a lost calf bawling
For the mud flanks of the cow. Stand
Gentle in my words. I saw the darkness
Tremble. I heard the darkness singing.

Tell you, darkness was pierced by the rose
Which vanished in a sun. Tell you, it was
A sun of glory the singing rose was
Saying. From the rose to the woman
From the woman to the man. From the man
To the sun. From the sun to the earth,
Beasts, and all creeping things. And the singing
Rose sang in the lap of Mary. Darkness
Sang to the light and the kiss of love was peace.

WILFRED WATSON
(1911–   )

Flower, Tree, and Bird

Glow, lonely heart,
alone with the hour.
She waits in the shadow:
pain, the dark flower.

Now stretches its branches
suffering's tree,

where sings in the green leaf
the bird, eternity.

Pain's blossom is silent,
her speech is gone.
The tree grows toward heaven,
and the bird sings on.

HERMANN HESSE
(1877–1962)
Translated from the German by
Herman Salinger

V

THE DISCIPLE
AND THE MASTER

If anyone wishes to come after me, let him deny himself, and take up his cross daily, and follow me. For he who would save his life will lose it; but he who loses his life for my sake will find it.

SAINT LUKE 9:23

The Mother of Sorrows, weeping, stood
Close to her Son beneath the rood
Where crucified He hung.

From *Stabat Mater*, ROMAN BREVIARY
(13th century)

THE FIRST FOLLOWERS

[*The commander of the temple and his men*] *brought* [*the apostles*] *before the council and the high priest questioned them.*

"We strictly forbade you," he said, "to teach on this authority, and here you have filled Jerusalem with your teaching, and propose to hold us responsible for this man's death!"

Peter and the apostles answered, "We must obey God rather than men. The God of our forefathers raised Jesus to life when you had hung him on a tree and killed him. God took him up to his right hand as leader and savior, in order to give repentance and forgiveness of sins to Israel. We and the holy Spirit which God has given to those who obey him are witnesses to these things."

When they heard this, they were furious, and wanted to kill them. But a Pharisee named Gamaliel, a teacher of the Law highly regarded by all the people, got up in the council and ordered the men to be removed for a while, and then said, "Men of Israel, take care what you propose to do with these men. For some time ago Theudas appeared, claiming to be a person of importance, and a group of men numbering some four hundred joined him. But he was killed and all his followers were dispersed and disappeared. After him, at the time of the census, Judas of Galilee appeared, and raised a following, but he too perished, and all his followers were scattered. So in the present case, I tell you, keep away from these men and let them alone, for if this idea or movement is of human origin, it will come to naught, but if it is from God, you will not be able to stop it. You may actually find yourselves fighting God!"

They were convinced by him, and they called the apostles in and had them flogged, and warned them not to speak about the name of Jesus, and then let them go. So they went out from before the council, glad that they had been thought worthy to bear disgrace for the sake of Jesus, and they did not for a single day stop teaching and preaching in the Temple and in private houses the good news of Jesus, the Christ.

ACTS OF THE APOSTLES 5:27–42

The Royal Road of the Holy Cross

In the cross is salvation, in the cross is life, in the cross is protection from enemies, in the cross is infusion of heavenly sweetness, in the cross is strength of mind, in the cross is joy of spirit, in the cross is highest virtue, in the cross is perfect holiness. There is no salvation of soul nor hope of everlasting life but in the cross.

Take up your cross, therefore, and follow Jesus, and you shall enter eternal life. He Himself opened the way before you in carrying His cross, and upon it He died for you, that you, too, might take up your cross and long to die upon it. If you die with Him, you shall also live with Him, and if you share His suffering, you shall also share His glory.

THOMAS À KEMPIS
(1380–1471)

Mary's Cross

Mary is the Mother of God, but her maternity was not without cross or grace. It would be a paradox of the love and wisdom of her Son to have a Mother who was not filled with grace, but in view of His design to die for men, it would have been repugnant for her to be His Mother and not have a mind and heart saturated with sorrows. As Mary drew close to divinity, through the sacred humanity which she gave her Son, it follows that although her grace was not a sharing of the personal grace of her Son, she had a very particular affinity to it. Finally, this grace had to be characterized by an inclination to the cross; not by a simple sharing of it, as is the case of the saints, but by a special affinity which was proper to her and could not be communicated to any other creature.

Mary belonged to Jesus' cross in a way different from that of the saints. They are said to be imitators and bearers of the cross; she was to burden Him with a cross more painful to Him than the one upon which He was to die. In becoming His Mother she became the occasion of Jesus' martyrdom.

Mary's affinity for the cross of Jesus consisted in this: in becoming His Mother, she was the principle of His cross in that human nature which she gave Him. She was His first cross; in her He offered His first sacrifice and began His experience of suffering and pain.

The grace which other men receive does not elevate them to a divine affinity but holds them to the order of participation. It does not dispose them to become so many crosses for Him, but inclines them only to bear them in imitation and to feel them by compassion. But it was not enough that Mary suffer with Christ; she attained the glory of her maternity by assuming the obligation to provide her Son's cross, for the Son of God was incapable of pain until He became the Son of man. Grace disposes one for the task to which he is called, and Mary was chosen to be God's Mother in a flesh in which He could experience pain. By her grace, then, Mary contracted an affinity to her Son's cross as well as to His uncreated Person. As His Mother she had also to be His cross.

No pure creature could ever attain a higher grace than to be the Mother of God; on the other hand, there is no affliction more cruel than for one close to God to be a cross for God.

Louis Chardon
(1595–1651)

My Love is Crucified

Neither the farthest reaches of this world shall profit me anything, nor shall its kingdoms. I would rather die for Jesus Christ than reign over the remotest realms of the earth. I seek Him who died for us; I desire Him who for our sake rose again. The pangs of a new birth are upon me. Forgive me, brethren. Do not keep me from this new life; do not desire my death. Do not give to the world one who so longs for God, nor tempt me with material things. Let me receive the pure light. When I have reached it, then shall I be a mature man. Permit me to be a follower of the passion of my God. If any possess Him, let them know my desires and share my feelings with me, for the things which urge me they will understand.

The prince of this world is ready to tear me to pieces and to weaken my will which is fixed on God. Let none of you, therefore, who look on at the conflict, abet him. Be on my side, rather, for that is the side of God. Do not have Jesus Christ on your lips and desire the world in your heart. Never let envy find a place in you. Even if I myself, when I am with you, should entreat you, do not obey me, but rather give your assent to what I write you now. I write to you in the fullness of life, yet longing for death. My love has been crucified, and there is no fire of material longing in me, but only living water speaking in me, saying, Come to the Father. I take no pleasure in the food of corruption or in the delights of this life. I desire the bread of God, which is the flesh of Christ who was of the seed of David; and for drink I desire His blood which is love that will not perish.

I write to all the churches, for I would have all know that I, of my own free will, die for God. . . . I exhort you, do not be unseasonably kind to me. Let me be given to the wild beasts, for through them I can reach God. I am God's wheat, and I am ground by the teeth of wild beasts that I may be found pure bread of Christ. Rather entice the wild beasts, that they may become my sepulchre and may leave no part of me, so that I may not, when I am fallen asleep, be a burden to you. Then shall I be indeed a disciple of Jesus Christ, when the world shall not so much as see my body. Petition the Lord for me, that through these instruments I may be found a sacrifice to God. I do not command you as Peter and Paul did. They were apostles; I am a convict. They were freemen, but I am a slave to this very hour. Yet if I shall suffer, then am I a freed-man of Christ Jesus, and I shall rise free in Him. Now in bondage I am learning to put away every desire.

SAINT IGNATIUS OF ANTIOCH
(martyred 215)

God as Teacher and Saviour

And now the learner, has he no lot or part in this story of suffering, even though his lot cannot be that of the Teacher? Aye, it cannot be otherwise. And the cause of all this suffering is love, precisely because God is not jealous for himself, but desires in love to be the equal of the humblest. When the seed of the oak is planted in earthen vessels they break asunder; when new wine is poured in old leathern bottles they burst; what must happen when God implants himself in human weakness, unless man becomes a new vessel and a new creature! But this becoming, what labors will attend the change, how convulsed with birth-pangs! And the understanding—how precarious, and how close each moment to misunderstanding, when the anguish of guilt seeks to disturb the peace of love! And how wrapt in fear; for it is indeed less terrible to fall to the ground when the mountains tremble at the voice of God, than to sit at table with him as an equal; and yet it is God's concern precisely to have it so.

SÖREN KIERKEGAARD
(1813–1855)

Mediocrity and the Cross

The deepest cause of our failures is that we have a superficial polish of Christian virtue but not its essence; we are too good to succeed in the world, but not good enough to overcome it. We are unable to follow great realists of nihilism like Machiavelli or Nietzsche, and so we get defeated. But let us follow Christ to the very end—to the Cross—and we shall be conquerors. This is the meaning of the mysterious promise given in the Gospels: "Blessed are the meek, for they shall inherit the earth." But we shall only be conquerors of the world when we have conquered ourselves sufficiently by means of the Person who Himself conquered the world.

GUSTAVE THIBON
(1904–   )

Rainbow

It was the hour when night makes the mountains lament
And the crags creak under the footsteps of animals,
The birds flew away from the countryside like poison
To get to the sea, to get to a better horizon.

Pursuing a poet then the devil went.
The poet stared at the sea as if he were dead,
For there the sea powdered the edge of a bay
And covered the skin of the giant rocks with scales.
But Jesus, with fire shining behind his head,
Came to climb up the black crags, bearing the cross.
The poet stretched out his arms towards the Savior
And everything vanished: the somber night and the beasts.
The poet followed God for his happiness.

MAX JACOB
(1876–1944)
*Translated from the French by
Elizabeth Bishop*

Pastorale

Shepherd who woke me from sleep piping of love,
You whose staff is made of that wood
Whereon your arms are outstretched,
Let your eyes of brooding compassion look on my faith.
I own you my lover and lord,
Proffer the pledge of my word
To follow forever
The flute and the beauteous feet.

Listen, shepherd dying of love:
For that you are friend of the fallen
My sin ought not to affright you.

Stay, then; hear the tale of my care.
Yet why should I ask you to tarry—
You whose feet, for waiting, are nailed?

Lopé de Vega
(1562–1635)
English version of the Spanish by
Sister Mary Immaculate, C.S.C.

God Spoke to Me

God said to me, "My son, you must love me. You see
My pierced side, my bleeding heart with its raying light,
And my bruised feet which Magdalene bathed
With her tears, and my arms stretched out under the weight

Of your sins, and my hands. And you see the cross,
You see the nails, the gall, the sponge; all teach you,
In this bitter world where flesh is king, to love only
My flesh and my blood, my voice and my word.
Have I not loved you, I myself, even unto death,
O my brother in my Father, O my son in the Holy Spirit,
And have I not suffered, even as it was written?

Have I not endured your own anguish,
Sweated, in your dark nights, your sweat of blood,
O unhappy friend seeking me here where I am?

Paul Verlaine
(1844–1896)
Translated from the French by
Sister Mary Immaculate, C.S.C.

From The Dialogue of Comfort

ANTHONY:[1] In bearing the loss of worldly goods, in suffering captivity, thraldom, and imprisonment, and in the glad sustaining of worldly shame, if we would in all those points deeply ponder the example of our Saviour himself, it would be sufficient of itself alone to encourage every true Christian man and woman to refuse none of all those calamities for his sake.

So say I now for painful death also: If we could and would with due compassion conceive in our minds a right imagination and remembrance of Christ's bitter painful passion—of the many sore bloody strokes that the cruel tormentors gave him with rods and whips upon every part of his holy tender body; of the scornful crown of sharp thorns beaten down upon his holy head, so strait and so deep that on every part his blessed blood issued out and streamed down; of his lovely limbs drawn and stretched out upon the cross, to the intolerable pain of his sore-beaten veins and sinews, feeling anew, with the cruel stretching and straining, pain far surpassing any cramp in every part of his blessed body at once; of the great long nails then cruelly driven with the hammer through his holy hands and feet; of his body, in this horrible pain, lifted up and let hang, with all its weight bearing down upon the painful wounded places so grievously pierced with nails; and in such torment, without pity, but not without many despites, suffered to be pinned and pained the space of more than three long hours, till he himself willingly gave up unto his Father his holy soul; after which yet, to show the mightiness of their malice, after his holy soul departed, they pierced his holy heart with a sharp spear, at which issued out the holy blood and water, whence his holy sacraments have inestimable secret strength—if we could, I

---

[1] Thomas More identified himself with Anthony.

say, remember these things, in such a way as would God that we would, I verily suppose that the consideration of his incomparable kindness could not fail so to inflame our key-cold hearts, and set them on fire with his love, that we should find ourselves not only content but also glad and desirous to suffer death for his sake who so marvellous lovingly forbore not to sustain so far passing painful death for ours. . . .

Oh, if he who is content to die for his love, of whom he looketh afterward for no reward, and yet by his death goeth from her, might by his death be sure to come to her and ever after in delight and pleasure to dwell with her—such a love would not stint here to die for her twice! And what cold lovers are we then unto God, if, rather than die for him once, we will refuse him and forsake him forever—him who both died for us before, and hath also provided that, if we die here for him, we shall in heaven everlastingly both live and also reign with him! For as St. Paul saith, "If we suffer with him, we shall reign with him."

SAINT THOMAS MORE
(1478–1535)

The Thief

"Say, bold blessed thief,
That in a trice
Slipped into paradise,
And in plain day
Stol'st heaven away,
What trick couldst thou invent
To compass thy intent?
What arms?

What charms?"
"Love and belief."

"Say, bold but blessed thief,
How couldst thou read
A crown upon that head?
What text, what gloss,
A kingdom and a cross?
How couldst thou come to spy
God in a man to die?
What light?
What sight?"
"The sight of grief."

"I sight to God his pain;
And by that sight
I saw the light;
Thus did my grief
Beget relief.
And take this rule from me,
Pity thou him he'll pity thee.
Use this,
Ne'er miss,
Heaven may be stol'n again."

ANONYMOUS
(17th century)

To Christ Crucified

My God, I am not moved to love Thee
By the heaven that Thou hast promised me,
Nor does the fear of hell move me
To leave off offending Thee.

Thou movest me, Lord. I am moved to see Thee
Nailed to that cross, and mocked.
Thy wounded body moves me.
I am moved by the anguish of Thy death.
I am moved, in a word, by Thy love, in such a way
That though there were no heaven I still should love Thee,
And though there were no hell, I still should fear Thee.
Thou needest give me no reason to love Thee, Lord,
For though I did not hope for all I hope for
I still should love Thee as I love Thee now.

ANONYMOUS
(16th century)
Translated from the Spanish by
Sister M. Katharine Elaine, C.S.C.

Saint

Struck into a mountain, one black cross
Speaks the martyrdom of your last hour,
And the pilgrim mourns the ancient loss,
Proffering his sorrow in a flower.

Here, where the foul plague once rioted,
Dying lips invoked your name and glory,
And steps only later steps have hid
Came in awe to learn your healing story.

Holy water seethed in font and bowl,
And the temple veil rent to derision,

But before your comprehending soul
Passed the sacred rood's triumphant vision.

Ah, your soul is out of reach of those
Who have sought your robes and dead belongings.
You are like a child whose dreaming knows
Even raindrops harbour deathless longings.

Seas subside and cleave at your approach,
And the foam spreads out in calm surrender.
Round about your path the ranks encroach,
Marshalled in the grace of angel splendour.

KERSTI MERILAAS
(1913–   )
Translated from the Estonian by
W. K. Matthews

The Martyrum Candidatus

Ah, see the fair chivalry come, the companions of Christ!
White Horsemen, who ride on white horses, the Knights of God!
They, for their Lord and their lover who sacrificed
All, save the sweetness of treading where He first trod!

These through the darkness of death, the dominion of night,
Swept, and they woke in white places at morning tide:
They saw with their eyes, and sang for joy of the sight,
They saw with their eyes the Eyes of the Crucified.

Now withersoever He goeth, with Him they go:
White Horsemen, who ride on white horses, oh fair to see!

They ride, where the Rivers of Paradise flash and flow,
White Horsemen, with Christ their Captain: for ever He!

LIONEL JOHNSON
(1867–1902)

Of Helena's Discovery

The Holy Places have been alternately honoured and desecrated,
lost and won, bought and bargained for, throughout the centuries.
But the wood has endured. In splinters and shavings gorgeously
encased it has travelled the world over and found a joyous welcome
among every race. For it states a fact.

Hounds are checked, hunting wild. A horn calls clear through
the covert. Helena casts them back on the scent.[1]

Above all the babble of her age and ours, she makes one blunt
assertion. And there alone is Hope.

EVELYN WAUGH
(1903–   )

The Stigmata of Saint Francis
From The Little Flowers of St. Francis

The day before the Feast of the Most Holy Cross, as St. Francis
was praying secretly in his cell, an angel of God appeared to him,

---

[1] Waugh's novel *Helena* is based on the tradition of the discovery of the true
Cross by St. Helena. For a note on the tradition, see above, pages 112-113.

and spake to him thus from God: "I am come to admonish and encourage thee, that thou prepare thyself to receive in all patience and humility that which God will give and do to thee."

St. Francis replied: "I am ready to bear patiently whatsoever my Lord shall be pleased to do to me"; and so the angel departed. On the following day—being the Feast of the Holy Cross—St. Francis was praying before daybreak at the entrance of his cell, and turning his face towards the east, he prayed in these words: "O Lord Jesus Christ, two graces do I ask of thee before I die; the first, that in my lifetime I may feel, as far as possible, both in my soul and body, that pain which thou, sweet Lord, didst endure in the hour of thy most bitter Passion; the second, that I may feel in my heart as much as possible of that excess of love by which thou, O Son of God, wast inflamed to suffer so cruel a Passion for us sinners." And continuing a long time in that prayer, he understood that God had heard him, and that, so far as is possible for a mere creature, he should be permitted to feel these things.

Having then received this promise, St. Francis began to contemplate most devoutly the Passion of Jesus Christ and his infinite charity; and so greatly did the fervour of devotion increase within him, that he was all transformed into Jesus by love and compassion.

And being thus inflamed in that contemplation, on that same morning he beheld a seraph descending from heaven with six fiery and resplendent wings; and this seraph with rapid flight drew nigh unto St. Francis, so that he could plainly discern him, and perceive that he bore the image of one crucified; and the wings were so disposed, that two were spread over the head, two were outstretched in flight, and the other two covered the whole body. And when St. Francis beheld it, he was much afraid, and filled at once with joy and grief and wonder. He felt great joy at the gracious presence of Christ, who appeared to him thus familiarly, and looked upon him thus lovingly, but, on the other hand, beholding him thus crucified, he felt exceeding grief and compassion. He marvelled much at so stupendous and unwonted a vision, knowing well that the infirmity of the Passion accorded ill with the immortality of the seraphic spirit. And in that perplexity of mind it was revealed to him by him who thus appeared, that by divine providence this vision had been thus shown to him that he might understand that, not by martyrdom of the body, but by a consuming fire of the soul, he was to be transformed into the express image of Christ crucified in that wonderful apparition. Then did all the Mount Alvernia appear wrapped in intense fire, which illumined all the mountains and valleys around, as it were the sun shining in his strength upon the earth, for which cause the shepherds who were watching their flocks in that country were filled with fear, as they themselves afterwards told the brethren, affirming that this light had been visible on Mount Alvernia for upwards of an hour. And because of the brightness of that light, which shone through the windows of the inn where they were tarrying, some muleteers who were travelling in Romagna arose in haste, supposing that the sun had risen, and saddled and loaded their beasts; but as they journeyed on, they saw that light disappear, and the visible sun arise.

In this seraphical apparition, Christ, who appeared under that form to St. Francis, spoke to him certain high and secret things, which in his lifetime he would never reveal to any person, but after his death he made them known to one of the brethren, and the words were these: "Knowest thou," said Christ, "what I have done to thee? I have given thee the stigmata which are the insignia of my Passion, that thou mayst be my standard-bearer; and as on the day of my death I descended into limbo, and by virtue of these my stigmata delivered thence all the souls whom I found there, so do I grant to thee that every year on the anniversary of thy death thou mayst go to purgatory, and take with thee to the glory of Paradise all the souls of thy three Orders, the Friars Minor, the Sisters, and the Penitents, and likewise all others whom thou shalt find there, who have been especially devout to thee; that so thou mayst be conformed to me in death, as thou has been like to me in life." Then, after long and secret conference together, that marvellous vision disappeared, leaving in the heart of St. Francis an excessive fire and ardour of divine love, and on his flesh a wonderful trace and image of the Passion of Christ. For upon his hands and feet began immediately to appear the figures of the nails as he had seen them on the Body of Christ crucified, who had appeared to him in the likeness of a seraph. And thus the hands and feet appeared pierced through the midst by the nails, the heads whereof were seen outside the flesh in the palms of the hands and the soles of the feet, and the points of the nails stood out at the back of the hands and the feet in such wise that they appeared to be twisted and bent back upon themselves, and the portion thereof that was bent back or twisted stood out free from the flesh, so that one could put a finger through the same as through a ring; and the heads of the nails were round and black. In like manner, on the right side appeared the image of an unhealed wound, as if made by a lance, and still red and bleeding, from which drops of blood often flowed from the holy breast of St. Francis, staining his tunic and his undergarment.

And because of this his companions, before they knew the truth from himself, perceiving that he would not uncover his hands and his feet, and that he could not set the soles of his feet upon the ground, and finding traces of blood upon his tunic when they washed it, understood of a certainty that he bore in his hands and feet and side the image and similitude of our Lord Jesus Christ crucified. And although he laboured hard to conceal these sacred stigmata holy and glorious, thus clearly impressed upon his flesh, yet finding that he could with difficulty hide them from his familiar companions, and fearing at the same time to reveal the secrets of God, he was in great doubt and trouble of mind whether or not he should make known the seraphical vision and the impression of the sacred, holy stigmata. At last, being pricked in conscience, he called together certain of the brethren, in whom he placed the greatest confidence, and proposing to them his doubt in general terms, asked their counsel on the matter. Now among these friars there was one of great sanctity, called Brother Illuminato; and he, being truly illuminated by God, understood that St. Francis must have seen something miraculous, and said thus to him: "Know, Brother Francis, that not for thyself alone, but for others, doth God reveal to thee his secrets, and therefore thou hast cause for fear lest thou be worthy of censure if thou conceal that which, for the good of others, has been made known to thee."

Then St. Francis, being moved by these words, with great fear and reverence told them the manner of the aforesaid vision, adding that Christ, who had thus appeared to him, had said to him certain things which he might never make known so long as he should live.

ANONYMOUS
(13th century)

When Mountain-ash in Clusters Reddens

When mountain-ash in clusters reddens,
Its leafage wet and stained with rust,
When through my palm the nail that deadens
By bony hands is shrewdly thrust,

When leaden-rippling rivers freeze me,
As on the wet gray height I toss,

While my austere-faced country sees me
Where I am swinging on the cross,

Then through my bloody agonizing
My staring eyes, with tears grown stiff,
Shall see on the broad river rising
Christ moving toward me in a skiff.

And in his eyes the same hopes biding,
And the same rags from him will trail,
His garment piteously hiding
The palm pierced with the final nail.

Christ! Saddened are the native reaches.
The cross tugs at my failing might.
Thy skiff—will it achieve these beaches,
And land here at my cruciate height?

ALEXANDER BLOK
(1880–1921)
*Translated from the Russian by
C. M. Bowra*

Stigmata

Whose the flying hands, about me shedding
Fire, and leading me on passionate ways?
No sonorous stones my feet are treading,
But where vatic waters fill the days.
Piercing through the spirit, sharp pilasters
Rise, and candles sting the dark like bees.
Oh, the hearts that bloom like crimson asters,
Petalled with gold-bladed ecstasies!

Now the evening on the temple flinging
Patterned, carven crimson, shines and mourns.
Oh, the pale brow to the altar clinging,
Stung anew with stinging scarlet thorns!
The whole soul, high vaults and portals glowing,
Fear like incense swathes with dim blue bands:
Ah, I know you, sacred corals, growing
On the pierced palms of these outstretched hands.

MAXIMILIAN VOLOSHIN
(1877–1932)
Translated from the Russian by
Babette Deutsch and Avrahm Yarmolinsky

Upon the Crucifix

Now I have found thee I will evermore
Embrace this standard where thou sitts above,
Feed greedy eyes, and from hence never rove;
Suck hungry soul of this eternal store;
Issue my heart from thy two leaved door,
And let my lips from kissing not remove.
O that I were transformed into love,
And as a plant might spring upon this flower,
Like wandring ivy or sweet honey suckle:
How would I with my twine about it buckle,
And kiss his feet with my ambitious boughs,
And climb along upon his sacred breast,
And make a garland for his wounded brows:
Lord so I am, if here my thoughts may rest.

WILLIAM ALABASTER
(1567–1640)

A Revelation on True Servants

These servants of mine, . . . who nourish themselves at this table of holy desire, are blessed and full of grief, even as my only-begotten Son was, on the wood of the holy cross, because, while his flesh was in grief and torment, his soul was blessed through its union with the divine nature. In like manner these are blessed by the union of their holy desire towards me, clothed . . . in my sweet will, and they are full of grief through compassion for their neighbor, and because they afflict their own self-love, depriving it of sensual delights and consolations.

SAINT CATHERINE OF SIENA
(1347–1380)

Women as Christ's Followers

'Twas a woman that washed his feet with tears, and a woman that anointed his body to the burial. They were women that wept when he was going to the cross; and women that followed him from the cross, and that sat by his sepulcher when he was buried. They were women that were first with him at his resurrection-morn, and women that brought tiding first to his disciples that he was risen from the dead. Women therefore are highly favoured, and shew by these things that they are sharers with us in the grace of life.

JOHN BUNYAN
(1628–1688)

The Virgin Martyrs

Therefore come they, the crowding maidens,
Gertrude, Agnes, Prisca, Cecily,
Lucy, Thekla, Juliana,
　　Barbara, Agatha, Petronel.

And other maids whose names I have read not,
Names I have read and now record not,
But their soul and their faith were maimed not,
　　Worthy now of God's company.

Wandering through the fresh fields go they,
Gathering flowers to make them a nosegay,
Gathering roses red for the Passion,
　　Lilies and violets for love.

　　　　　　　SIGEBERT OF GEMBLOUX
　　　　　　　　　　(*c.* 1030–1112)
　　　　　　　Translated from the Latin by
　　　　　　　　　　Helen Waddell

A Revelation of Divine Love

In this [time of beholding the crucifix] I would have looked up
from the Cross, but I durst not. For I wist well that while I beheld
in the Cross I was sure and safe; therefore I would not assent to
put my soul in peril: for beside the Cross was no sureness, for fear
of fiends.

　　Then had I a proffer in my reason as [if] it had been friendly said to me: "Look up to Heaven to his Father." And then saw I well, with the faith that I felt, that there was nothing betwixt the Cross and Heaven that might have dis-eased me. Either me behoved to look up or else to answer. I answered inwardly with all the might of my soul, and said: "Nay; I may not: for thou art my Heaven." This I said for [that] I would not. For I would liever have been in that pain till Doomsday than to come to Heaven otherwise than by him. For I wist well that he that bound me so sore, he should unbind me when that he would. Thus was I learned to choose Jesus to my Heaven, whom I saw only in pain at that time: meliked no other Heaven than Jesus, which shall be my bliss when I come there.

And this hath ever been a comfort to me, that I chose Jesus to my Heaven, by his grace, in all this time of Passion and sorrow; and that hath been a learning to me that I should evermore do so: choosing only Jesus to my Heaven in weal and woe.

SAINT JULIANA OF NORWICH
(1343–1423)

From Troilus and Criseyde

O yonge, fresshe folkes, he or she,
In which that love up groweth with youre age,
Repeyreth hom fro worldly vanyte,
And of youre herte up casteth the visage
To thilke God that after his ymage
Yow made, and thynketh al nys but a faire
This world, that passeth soone as floures faire.

And loveth hym, the which that right for love
Upon a crois, oure soules for to beye,

First starf, and roos, and sit in hevene above;
For he nyl falsen no wight, dar I seye,
That wol his herte al holly on hym leye.
And syn he best to love is, and most meke,
What nedeth feynede loves for to seke?

GEOFFREY CHAUCER
(1340?–1400)

O young, fresh folk, boys or girls, in whom love grows with your years, from
worldly vanity go home. Let your heart turn its face to that same God who
made you after His image, and think all else is nothing but a fair, and passes
as quickly as the lovely flowers. Love Him, who truly for love, on the cross, to redeem our souls, first died, and rose, and sits in heaven above; for He will betray
no creature, I make bold to say, who with his whole heart leans on Him. And
since He of all lovers is best, and most gentle, what need is there to seek false
loves?

The Canterbury Pilgrims[1]

honour corruption villainy holiness
riding in fragrance of sunlight (side by side
all in a singing wonder of blossoming yes
riding) to him who died that death should be dead

humblest and proudest eagerly wandering
(equally all alive in miraculous day)
merrily moving through sweet forgiveness of spring
(over the under the gift of the earth of the sky

knight and ploughman pardoner wife and nun
merchant frere clerk somnour miller and reve

---

[1] Editor's title.

and geoffrey and all) come up from the never of when
come into the now of forever come riding alive

down while crylessly drifting through vast most
nothing's own nothing children go of dust

E. E. CUMMINGS
(1894–1962)

The Duty Today

There never was a time . . . when the salvation of souls did not
impose on all the duty of associating their sufferings with the
torments of our divine Redeemer. But today that duty is clearer
than ever when a gigantic conflict has set almost the whole world
on fire, and leaves in its wake so much death, so much misery, so
much sorrow. Today imposes with particular stress on everyone
the duty to flee the vices and blandishments of the world, and to
renounce the unrestrained pleasures of the body and that worldly
frivolity and vanity which contribute nothing to the Christian
formation of the soul, nothing towards gaining heaven. Rather let
those words of Our immortal predecessor Leo the Great be deeply
engraven in our minds, that Baptism has made us flesh of the
Crucified One; and that beautiful prayer of St. Ambrose: "Carry
me, Christ, on the Cross, which is salvation to the wanderers, sole
rest for the wearied, wherein alone is life for those who die."

POPE PIUS XII
(1876–1958)

The Recollection and the Blood of the Lamb
From The Sound and the Fury

When the visitor rose to speak he sounded like a white man.[1] His voice was level and cold. It sounded too big to have come from him and they listened at first through curiosity, as they would have to a monkey talking. They began to watch him as they would a man on a tight rope. They even forgot his insignificant appearance in the virtuosity with which he ran and poised and swooped upon the cold inflectionless wire of his voice, so that at last, when with a sort of swooping glide he came to rest again beside the reading desk with one arm resting upon it at shoulder height and his monkey body as reft of all motion as a mummy or an emptied vessel, the congregation sighed as if it waked from a collective dream and moved a little in its seats. Behind the pulpit the choir fanned steadily. Dilsey whispered, "Hush, now. Dey fixin to sing in a minute."

Then a voice said, "Brethren."

The preacher had not moved. His arm lay yet across the desk, and he still held that pose while the voice died in sonorous echoes between the walls. It was as different as day and dark from his former tone, with a sad, timbrous quality like an alto horn, sinking into their hearts and speaking there again when it had ceased in fading and cumulate echoes.

"Brethren and sisteren," it said again. . . . "I got the recollection and the blood of the Lamb." He tramped steadily back and forth beneath the twisted paper and the Christmas bell, hunched, his hands clasped behind him. . . . And the congregation seemed to watch with its own eyes while the voice consumed him, until he

---

[1] In *The Sound and the Fury*, Dilsey, the Negro servant, has taken Benjy, her retarded charge, to a church service with her.

was nothing and they were nothing and there was not even a voice but instead their hearts were speaking to one another in chanting measures beyond the need for words, so that when he came to rest against the reading desk, his monkey face lifted and his whole attitude that of a serene, tortured crucifix that transcended its shabbiness and insignificance and made it of no moment, a long moaning expulsion of breath rose from them, and a woman's single soprano: "Yes, Jesus!"

As the scudding day passed overhead the dingy windows glowed and faded in ghostly retrograde. A car passed along the road outside, labouring in the sand, died away. Dilsey sat bolt upright, her hand on Ben's knee. Two tears slid down her fallen cheeks, in and out of the myriad coruscation of immolation and abnegation and time.

"Brethren," the minister said in a harsh whisper, without moving.

"Yes, Jesus!" the woman's voice said, hushed yet.

"Breddren and sistuhn!" His voice rang again, with the horns. He removed his arm and stood erect and raised his hands. "I got de ricklickshun en de blood of de Lamb!" They did not mark just when his intonation, his pronunciation, became negroid, they just sat swaying a little in their seats as the voice took them into itself.

"When de long, cold—Oh, I tells you, breddren, when de long, cold—I sees de light en I sees de word, po sinner! Dey passed away in Egypt, de swingin chariots; de generations passed away. Wus a rich man: whar he now, O breddren? Was a po man: whar he now, O sistuhn? Oh I tells you, ef you aint got de milk en de dew of de old salvation when de long, cold years rolls away!"

"Yes, Jesus!"

"I tells you, breddren, en I tells you, sistuhn, dey'll come a time. Po sinner saying Let me lay down wid de Lawd, lemme lay down my load. Den whut Jesus gwine say, O breddren? O sistuhn? Is you got de ricklickshun en de blood of de Lamb? Case I aint gwine load down heaven!"

He fumbled in his coat and took out a handkerchief and mopped his face. A low concerted sound rose from the congregation: "Mmmmmmmmmmmmmm!" The woman's voice said, "Yes, Jesus! Jesus!"

"Breddren! Look at dem little chillen settin dar. Jesus was like dat once. He mammy suffered de glory en de pangs. Sometime maybe she helt him at de nightfall, whilst de angels singin him to sleep; maybe she look out de do' en see de Roman po-lice passin." He tramped back and forth, mopping his face. "Listen, breddren! I sees de day. Ma'y settin in de do' wid Jesus on her lap, de little Jesus. Like dem chillen dar, de little Jesus. I hears de angels singin de peaceful songs en de glory; I sees de closin eyes; sees Mary jump up, sees de sojer face: We gwine to kill! We gwine to kill! We gwine to kill yo little Jesus! I hears de weepin en de lamentation of de po mammy widout de salvation en de word of God!"

"Mmmmmmmmmmmmmmm! Jesus! Little Jesus!" and another voice rising:

"I sees, O Jesus! Oh I sees!" and still another, without words, like bubbles rising in water.

"I sees hit, breddren! I sees hit! Sees de blastin, blindin sight! I sees Calvary, wid de sacred trees, sees de thief en de murderer en de least of dese; I hears de boasting en de braggin: Ef you be Jesus, lif up yo tree en walk! I hear de wailin of women en de evenin lamentations; I hears de weepin en de crying en de turnt-away face of God: dey done kilt Jesus; de done kilt my Son."

"Mmmmmmmmmmmmmmm. Jesus! I sees, O Jesus!"

"O blind sinner! Breddren, I tells you; sistuhn, I says to you when de Lawd did turn His mighty face, say, Aint gwine overload heaven! I can see de widowed God shet His do'; I sees de whelmin flood roll between; I sees de darkness en de death everlastin upon de generations. Den, lo! Breddren! Yes, breddren! Whut I see, Whut I see, O sinner: I sees de resurrection en de light; sees de meek Jesus saying Dey kilt Me dat ye shall live again; I died dat dem whut sees en believes shall never die. Breddren, O breddren! I sees de doom crack en hears de golden horns shoutin down de glory, en de arisen dead whut got de blood en de ricklickshun of de Lamb!"

In the midst of the voices and hands Ben sat, rapt in his sweet blue gaze. Dilsey sat bolt upright beside, crying rigidly and quietly in the annealment and the blood of the remembered Lamb.

As they walked through the bright noon, up the sandy road with the dispersing congregation talking easily again group to group, she continued to weep, unmindful of the talk.

"He sho a preacher, mon! He didn't look like much at first, but hush!"

"He seed de power en de glory."

"Yes, suh. He seed hit. Face to face he seed hit."

Dilsey made no sound, her face did not quiver as the tears took their sunken and devious courses, walking with her head up, making no effort to dry them away even.

"Whyn't you quit dat, mammy?" Frony said. "Wid all dese people lookin. We be passin white folks soon."

"I've seed de first en de last," Dilsey said. "Never you mind me."

"First en last whut?" Frony said.

"Never you mind," Dilsey said. "I seed de beginnin, en now I sees de endin."

WILLIAM FAULKNER
(1897–1962)

VI

THE SIGN OF CONTRADICTION

And Simeon . . . said to Mary his mother,
"Behold, this child is destined for the fall and
for the rise of many in Israel, and for a sign
that shall be contradicted."

SAINT LUKE 2:34

I have come not to bring peace but a sword.

SAINT MATTHEW 10:34

HE WAS WOUNDED
FOR OUR REBELLIONS

Who would have believed our report?
And the arm of Jahweh, upon whom was it revealed?
And he grew up before Him like a sapling,
And like a root from arid land;
No beauty had he,
No majesty that we should regard him,
And no comeliness that we should delight in him;
He was despised and aloof from men,
A man of pains and familiar with suffering,
And as one who hid his face from us
He was despised and we esteemed him not.

But it was our sufferings that he bore,
Our pains that he endured;
And we accounted him stricken,
Smitten by God and afflicted,
But he was wounded for our rebellions,
He was bruised for our sins;
Upon him was the chastisement which made us whole,
And by his stripes we were healed.

We all like sheep had gone astray,
We had turned each his own way,
And Jahweh made to light upon him
The iniquities of us all;

He was afflicted, but he was resigned,
And he opened not his mouth;
Like a lamb that is led to the slaughter,
And like a ewe that is dumb before its shearers,
Without stay and without judgment was he taken,
And his latter end, who could conceive?

For he was cut off from the land of the living,
With the rebellious who are stricken down,
And his grave was assigned among the wicked,
And his portion with the doers of evil,
Albeit he had done no violence,
And there was no deceit in his mouth,
And Jahweh was pleased to crush him with suffering;‖
Though his own life be made a sin-offering,
He shall see a seed that shall have length of days,
And the purpose of Jahweh shall prosper in his hand.

Because of his soul's sorrow he shall see it,
Through his suffering he shall be filled;
A righteous one, My servant, shall make many righteous,
And their iniquities he shall bear;
Therefore will I give him a portion with the mighty,
And with the powerful shall he divide the spoil;
Because he shall have poured out his soul to death,
And been numbered with the rebellious,
So shall he take away the sins of many,
And make intercession for the rebellious.

ISAIAS 53:1–12
(written *c.* 740–701 B.C.)

The Pilgrim of the Absolute

Suffering! here then is the key word! Here the solution for every human life on earth! the springboard for every superiority, the sieve for every merit, the infallible criterion for every moral beauty! People absolutely refuse to understand that suffering is needful. Those who say that suffering is useful understand nothing about the matter. Usefulness always supposes something adjectival and contingent, and Suffering is *necessary*. It is the backbone, the very essence of moral life. Love is recognized by this sign, and when this sign is lacking, love is but a prostitution of strength or of beauty. I say that someone loves me when that someone consents to suffer through or for me. . . .

Well, we are—what, Lord God?—yes, we are the MEMBERS of Jesus Christ! His very members! Our unutterable wretchedness comes from our continually taking for figures or inanimate symbols the clearest and most living assertions of the Scriptures. We believe, but not *substantially*. Ah! the words of the Holy Ghost should enter and flow through our souls as did molten lead in the mouth of a parricide or a blasphemer. We do not understand that we are the members of the *Man of Sorrows*, of the Man who is supreme Joy, Love, Truth, Beauty, Light and Life solely because He is the Lover eternally stricken with the supreme Suffering, the Pilgrim of the last torment, who, to endure it, rushed up through infinity, from the far deep of eternity, and on whose head have been heaped in an appallingly tragic unity of time, place and person, all the elements of torture, collected from every human act performed during each second, over the whole surface of the earth, for the length of sixty centuries!

We can use this as a starting point to measure all things. In declaring us members of Jesus Christ, the Holy Spirit clothed us with the dignity of Redeemers, and, when we refuse to suffer, we are straitly guilty of simony and betrayal of trust. We have been made for that, and for that alone. When we shed our blood it flows on Calvary, and from thence over the whole earth. Woe to us, therefore, if this blood be poisoned! When we shed our tears, which are "the blood of our souls," they fall on the heart of the Virgin, and from there onto all living hearts. Our standing as members of Jesus Christ and sons of Mary has made us so great that we can drown the world in our tears. Woe, then, and three times woe upon us, if these tears are poisoned! Everything in us is identical with Jesus Christ, to whose likeness we have been naturally and supernaturally shaped. So when we refuse suffering, we adulterate as much as we are able our own substance; we cause to enter into the very Flesh and even the Soul of our Head, a profanating element which He must afterwards cast from Himself and all His members by an inconceivable redoubling of torment.

The Saints have sought the society of Jesus' Passion. They believed the saying of the Master when He said that he possesses the greatest love who gives his life for his friends. In all ages, ardent and magnificent souls have thought that in order *to do enough*, it was absolutely necessary *to do too much*, and that thus did one ravish the Kingdom of the Heavens. . . . It is wholly certain that the humblest among the oppressed will in the end be avenged and in the end consoled, when will come the hour of the infallible retributions. We are on the rack only in order to avow Glory.

Do you know that to be a real Christian, that is to say a *Saint*, one must have a tender heart within a shell of bronze? Saint Luke tells that in the midst of the most unutterable suffering, Christ had pity on the brutes who were crucifying Him and that He entreated His Father to forgive them. "They know not what they do," He cried unto Him. Now remember that a filthy butcher or pig-sticker who, not satisfied with slaughtering his poor animals, unworthily and ridiculously mutilates them after their death, carries on—after a fashion—in the most unfathomable darknesses, the immolation of the Saviour, and that they are enfolded in His Prayer. All the more do they need it as they are more abject, more unfeeling, more snug in an appalling ignorance of what they do.

Christ is at the center of all things, He takes all things upon Himself, He bears all things, He suffers all things. It is impossible to strike a human being without striking Him, to humiliate someone without humiliating Him, curse or kill anyone without cursing Him or killing Him, Himself. The lowest of contemptible fellows is forced to borrow the Face of Christ in order to receive a blow, from no matter what hand. Otherwise the buffet could never reach him and would remain hanging in interstellar space, through the ages of ages, until it should have met with the Face which forgives. . . .

Léon Bloy
(1846–1917)

The Galilean

Yet one from Galilee   who did not say
"Kill them for treason   kill them for sabotage
Kill them that hinder my agrarian scheme
Exile and liquidate them who dispute

my view   my way!"
        In the Day of the Lie
withdraw the nails   support the body down. . .

and in the twilit garden   terribly
hushed   wash the body   take from off the head
the crown of scorns   and sprinkle all the body
with spice and tie it in a winding sheet. . .

"Woman, why weepest thou? Whom seekest thou?"

"Because I know not where. . ."

               "Mary!"
                      "Rabboni!"

. . . such dry-mouthed terror in that utter darkness
and now such light. . .

          outside the old walled city
of Caiaphas
          outside the old walled city
of Lutetia a town in Gaul
               outside the city
walled and called Londinium of old time. . .

Love one another
               . . . and the streams of blood. . .

The upper room   the wine   loaves without leaven
"This do in remembrance of me—!"

He took the cup. . .

"Lord is it I?"

. . . by whom the son of Man
is again betrayed

It had been good for him
If he had not been born   for he shall live
only forever with jackals of the night. . .
And after they had crucified Him
the Parthians revolted against the Legions
the Britons rebelled and massacred the Romans
Gaul rose   and Nero gabbled near his end
and the Spanish proclaimed Galba   and Nero fled
from the Golden House   and Galba entered Rome
but brought no peace   Soon the Praetorians killed him
and proclaimed Otho

and there was sound of war
on the Rhine   the Danube   the Po   the Tiber
the shore of the North Sea   Caligula
the incestuous epileptic screamed for earthquake
and pestilence   and Asia and Achaia
and Macedonia   and Naples   and Pompeii
shook with earthquake   and the whole Campagna
screamed for terror. . .

In the fulness of time
were the signs fulfilled. . .

But who shall mend for us
the fishers' nets on the Capernaum shore . . . ?

WILLIAM ROSE BENÉT
(1886–1950)

Ecce Homo

Whose is this horrifying face,
This putrid flesh, discoloured, flayed,
Fed on by flies, scorched by the sun?
Whose are these hollow red-filmed eyes
And thorn-spiked head and spear-stuck side?
Behold the Man: He is Man's Son.

Forget the legend, tear the decent veil
That cowardice or interest devised
To make their mortal enemy a friend,
To hide the bitter truth all His wounds tell,
Lest the great scandal be no more disguised:
He is in agony till the world's end,

And we must never sleep during that time!
He is suspended on the cross-tree now
And we are onlookers at the crime,
Callous contemporaries of the slow
Torture of God. Here is the hill
Made ghastly by His splattered blood.

Whereon He hangs and suffers still:
See, the centurions wear riding-boots,
Black shirts and badges and peaked caps,
Greet one another with raised-arm salutes;
They have cold eyes, unsmiling lips;
Yet these His brothers know not what they do.

And on His either side hang dead
A labourer and a factory hand,

Or one is maybe a lynched Jew
And one a Negro or a Red,
Coolie or Ethiopian, Irishman,
Spaniard or German democrat.

Behind his lolling head the sky
Glares like a fiery cataract
Red with the murders of two thousand years
Committed in His name and by
Crusaders, Christian warriors
Defending faith and property.

Amid the plain beneath His transfixed hands,
Exuding darkness as indelible
As guilty stains, fanned by funereal
And lurid airs, besieged by drifting sands
And clefted landslides our about-to-be
Bombed and abandoned cities stand.

He who wept for Jerusalem
Now sees His prophecy extend
Across the greatest cities of the world,
A guilty panic reason cannot stem
Rising to raze them all as He foretold;
And He must watch this drama to the end.

Though often named, He is unknown
To the dark kingdoms at His feet
Where everything disparages His words,
And each man bears the common guilt alone
And goes blindfolded to his fate,
And fear and greed are sovereign lords.

The turning point of history
Must come. Yet the complacent and the proud
And who exploit and kill, may be denied—
Christ of Revolution and of Poetry—
The resurrection and the life
Wrought by your spirit's blood.

Involved in their own sophistry
The black priest and the upright man
Faced by subversive truth shall be struck dumb,
Christ of Revolution and of Poetry,
While the rejected and condemned become
Agents of the divine.

Not from a monstrance silver-wrought
But from the tree of human pain
Redeem our sterile misery,
Christ of Revolution and of Poetry,
That man's long journey through the night
May not have been in vain.

DAVID GASCOYNE
(1916–   )

Still Falls the Rain
The Raids, 1940. Night and Dawn

Still falls the Rain—
Dark as the world of man, black as our loss—
Blind as the nineteen hundred and forty nails
Upon the Cross.

Still falls the Rain
With a sound like the pulse of the heart that is changed to the
  hammer beat
In Potter's Field, and the sound of the impious feet
On the Tomb:

Still falls the Rain
In the Field of Blood where the small hopes breed and the
  human brain
Nurtures its greed, that worm with the brow of Cain.

Still falls the Rain
At the feet of the Starved Man hung upon the Cross.
Christ that each day, each night, nails there, have mercy on us—
On Dives and on Lazarus:
Under the Rain the sore and the gold are as one.

Still falls the Rain—
Still falls the Blood from the Starved Man's wounded Side:
He bears in His Heart all wounds,—those of the light that died,
The last faint spark
In the self-murdered heart, the wounds of the sad
  uncomprehending dark,
The wounds of the baited bear,—
The blind and weeping bear whom the keepers beat
On his helpless flesh . . . the tears of the hunted hare.

Still falls the Rain—
Then—O Ile leape up to my God: who pulles me doune—
See, see where Christ's blood streames in the firmament:
It flows from the Brow we nailed upon the tree
Deep to the dying, to the thirsting heart
That holds the fires of the world,—dark-smirched with pain
As Caesar's laurel crown.

Then sounds the voice of One who like the heart of man
Was once a child who among beasts has lain—
"Still do I love, still shed my innocent light, my Blood, for thee."

EDITH SITWELL
(1887–1964)

The Barrier of Enmity

Christ crucified extends His arms toward both Jews and Gentiles; He died, Saint Paul says, in order to reconcile the two peoples, and to break down the dividing barrier of enmity between them. "For He is our peace, He that hath made both one, and hath broken down the dividing barrier of enmity. He hath brought to naught in His flesh the law of commandments framed in decrees, that in Himself He might create of the two one new man, and make peace and reconcile both in one body to God through the cross, slaying by means thereof their enmity."

If the Jewish people did not hear the call made to them by the dying Christ, yet do they remain ever summoned. If the Gentiles indeed heard the call, now racist paganism casts them away from it and from Him who is our peace. Anti-Semitic hatred is a directly anti-Christic frenzy to make vain the blood of Jesus and to make void His death. Reconciliation, breaking down the barrier of enmity—these, which the madness of men prevented love from accomplishing, and the frustration of which is the most refined torment in the sufferings of the Messiah—these agony now is the way of achieving, a universal agony in the likeness of that of the Saviour, both the agony of the racked, abandoned Jews and of the racked, abandoned Christians who live by faith.

More than ever, the mystical body of Christ needs the people of God. In the darkness of the present day, that moment seems invisibly to be in preparation, however remote it still may be, when their reintegration, as Saint Thomas puts it, will "call back to life the Gentiles, that is to say the lukewarm faithful, when 'on account of the progress of iniquity, the charity of a great number shall have waxed cold' " (Matt. xxiv.12).

JACQUES MARITAIN

(1882–   )

The Wounds of Today

On the second day of Lent, . . . I had just communicated, when Our Lord Jesus Christ appeared to me. . . . While I was looking at Him, I saw that, encircling His head, instead of the crown of thorns, in what must have been the place where He was wounded by it, was a crown of great splendor. As I am devoted to this mystery, I was very much comforted; and then I began to think what torture He must have suffered from the many wounds it gave Him and I felt very much distressed. Then the Lord told me not to be grieved because of those wounds but because of the many wounds inflicted upon Him now.

SAINT TERESA OF ÁVILA

(1515–1582)

An Argument: of the Passion of Christ

And what one of you, by taking thought,
can add to his stature one cubit?
Matt. vi.27

I

The furious prisoner of the womb,
Rebellious, in the jaws of life,
Learns, from the mother's conscious flesh,
The secret laws of blood and strife.

The demon raging at the breast,
Arrayed in cries, and crowned with tears,
Has sucked the magics of the east,
The doubts of the philosophers.

In the red straits of his arteries,
Love runs, lost and ravening;
Nothingness feeds upon itself
And swells up to a mighty king!

Wit walks out, in envy's mask;
Love will hide, and be a lecher.
Adultery, by taking thought,
Adds a cubit to his stature,

Until we scan the wastes of death,
And wind blows through our cage of bones;
Sight leaves the sockets of the skull,
And love runs mad among the stones!

I I

The worm that watched within the womb
Was standing guard at Jesus' tomb
And my first angry, infant breath
Stood wakeful, lest He rise from death.
My adolescence, like the wolf,
Fled to the edges of the gulf
And searched the ruins of the night
To hide from Calvary's iron light:
But in the burning jaws of day
I saw the barren Judas Tree;
For, to the caverns of my pride
Judas had come, and there was paid!

I I I

Seeds of the three hours' agony
Fell on good earth, and grew from me,
And, cherished by my sleepless cares
Flowered with God's Blood, and Mary's tears.
My curious love found its reward
When Love was scourged in Pilate's yard:
Here was the work my hands had made:
A thorny crown, to cut His head.
The growth of thoughts that made me great
Lay on His cross, and were its weight;
And my desires lay, turned to stones,
And where He fell, cut to the bone.
The sharpnesses of my delight
Were spikes run through His hands and feet,

And from the sweetness of my will
Their sponge drew vinegar and gall.

THOMAS MERTON
(1915–   )

The Mystery of Pain

Christianity, without ever a hesitation, from the first and every-where, refused to hold, or even to tolerate, either the one or the other of the two only attempts at self-persuasion which, then as now, possess souls that suffer whilst they have not yet found the deepest. Christianity refused all Epicureanism,—since man can-not find his deepest by fleeing from pain and suffering, and by seeking pleasure and pleasures, however dainty and refined. And it refused all Stoicism,—since pain, suffering, evil are not fancies and prejudices, but real, very real; and since man's greatest action and disposition is not self-sufficingness or aloofness, but self-donation and love. Christianity refuted these theories, not by means of another theory of its own, but simply by exhibiting a Life and lives—the Life of the Crucified, and lives which con-tinually re-live, in their endless various lesser degrees and ways, such a combination of gain in giving and of joy in suffering. Chris-tianity thus gave to souls the faith and strength to grasp life's nettle. It raised them, in their deepest dispositions and innermost will, above the pitiful oscillations and artificialities of even the greatest of the Pagans in this central matter,—between eluding, ignoring pain and suffering, and, animal-like, seeking life in its fleeting, momentary pleasures; or trying the nobler yet impossible course,—the making out that physical, mental, moral pain and evil are nothing real, and the suppressing of emotion, sympathy and pity as things unworthy of the adult soul. Christianity did neither. It pointed to Jesus with the terror of death upon Him in Gethsemane; with a cry of desolation upon the Cross on Calvary; it allowed the soul, it encouraged the soul to sob itself out. It not only taught men frankly to face and to recognize physical and mental pain, death, and all other, especially all moral evils and sufferings as very real; it actually showed men the presence and gravity of a host of pains, evils and miseries which they had, up to then, quite ignored or at least greatly minimized. And yet, with all this—in spite of all such material for despair the final note of Christianity was and is still, one of trust, of love, of transcendent joy. It is no accident, but of the very essence of the mystery and of the power of faith, it springs from the reality of God and of His action within men's souls, that, as the nobly joyous last chapters of Isaiah[1] contain also those wondrous utterances of the man of sorrows, so also the serenity of the Mount of the Beatitudes leads, in the Gospels, to the darkness of Calvary.

FRIEDERICH VON HÜGEL
(1852–1925)

You Are the Branches

Ah, Lord,
Thy vine still gives Thee vinegar to drink.

COVENTRY PATMORE
(1823–1896)

---

[1] Chapter xi to the end.

Monologue for the Good Friday Christ

The good Friday crowd went
In queues to kiss the crux
Fidelis; soon shall each
Have back to the least
Joy and red cent
What he gave up for Lent.

But christ what do we do
That hate pain and can't
Pray and are not able
Not to sin; that stay
Contrite, until night: did you
Not die for us too?

That will not move to welcome,
Or like The Baptist, leap
And so live; or cannot feed
Upon the quick and lean
Locust, are not at home
With the eyed and austere honeycomb?

Are not the nails sweet
The wood that held thy weight
And what other tree ever put
Such leaf or flower or root
But why am I here in my seat
By my sins and your defeat—

I shall read psalms and wait,
But why can I not kiss
The crucifix my lips

Are dry my tongue sticks
In my jaw oh come great
God as the early and the late

Rains come bind the thorn
From my soul the raged light
Lions from my flesh my sweets
Hold from the dog's hand let
My afflictions be not torn
On the turned spear of the unicorn

God God do not die
This afternoon, we but
Enact: but Christ rise
And before Easter light
In us new fire and spring
The cold, burned root of the old!

Our holy master has died;
We kneel and touch lips to our pride.

JOHN LOGAN
(1923–   )

With Mercy for the Greedy

For my friend, Ruth, who urges me to make an
appointment for the Sacrament of Confession

Concerning your letter in which you ask
me to call a priest and in which you ask
me to wear The Cross that you enclose;
your own cross,
your dog-bitten cross,

no larger than a thumb,
small and wooden, no thorns, this rose—

I pray to its shadow,
that gray place
where it lies on your letter . . . deep, deep.
I detest my sins and I try to believe
in The Cross. I touch its tender hips, its dark jawed face,
its solid neck, its brown sleep.

True. There is
a beautiful Jesus.
He is frozen to his bones like a chunk of beef.
How desperately he wanted to pull his arms in!
How desperately I touch his vertical and horizontal axes!
But I can't. Need is not quite belief.

All morning long
I have worn
your cross, hung with package string around my throat.
It tapped me lightly as a child's heart might,
tapping secondhand, softly waiting to be born.
Ruth, I cherish the letter you wrote.

My friend, my friend, I was born
doing reference work in sin, and born
confessing it. This is what poems are:
with mercy
for the greedy,
they are the tongue's wrangle,
the world's pottage, the rat's star.

ANNE SEXTON
(1928-   )

Place of a Skull

Earth water stars and flesh—the seamless coat
Which is the world, he left; who from to-day
Had no more need to wear it. The remote
Metropolis yawned, the parchment flapped away,

Away, and the blood dried in the sand. The bored
Soldiers played for the leavings but even they,
Though trained to carve up continents with the sword,
Approved the weaver who had made night and day

And time and mind a tegument, therefore swore
To hazard it as one lot. The dice were gay
And someone won: *Why the first time I wore*
That dead man's coat it frayed I cannot say.

LOUIS MACNEICE
(1907–1963)

The Crucifix

How dry time screaks in its fat axle-grease,
As spare November strikes us through the ice
And the Leviathan breaks water in the rice
Fields, at the poles, at the hot gates to Greece;
It's time: the old unmastered lion roars
And ramps like a mad dog outside the doors,

Snapping at gobbets in my thumbless hand.
The seaways lurch through Sodom's knees of sand
Tomorrow. We are sinking. "Run, rat, run,"
The prophets thunder, and I run upon
My father, Adam. Adam, if our land
Become the desolation of a hand
That shakes the Temple back to clay, how can
War ever change my old into new man?
Get out from under my feet, old man. Let me pass;
On Ninth Street, through the Hallowe'en's soaped glass,
I picked at an old bone on two crossed sticks
And found, to *Via et Vita et Veritas*
A stray dog's signpost is a crucifix.

ROBERT LOWELL
(1917–   )

The Cross

There is a place that some men know,
I cannot see the whole of it
Nor how I came there. Long ago
Flame burst out of a secret pit
Crushing the world with such a light
The day-sky fell to moonless black,
The kingly sun to hateful night
For those, once seeing, turning back:
For love so hates mortality
Which is the providence of life

She will not let it blessèd be
But curses it with mortal strife,
Until beside the blinding rood
Within that world-destroying pit
—Like young wolves that have tasted blood,
Of death, men taste no more of it.
So blind, in so severe a place
(All life before in the black grave)
The last alternatives they face
Of life, without the life to save,
Being from all salvation weaned—
A stag charged both at heel and head:
Who would come back is turned a fiend
Instructed by the fiery dead.

ALLEN TATE
(1899–   )

The Return[1]

They covered His body with linen
Then placed it in a tomb.
His women wept. And they
Who'd followed Him with more hopes than understanding
Immediately began to shift for themselves
Disappointed at the turn of events
Yet relieved at the same time since these
Now gave them no alternative but to return home:

---

[1] Editor's title; from *Judas*.

Peter to his fishing, it was the season for herring;
Andrew to his camels, two of them in foal.
Each had a claw in his heart, a home—
Something they could at least return to
And they made their preparations, forgetting
That though it is possible to lock a body in a tomb
It is not possible to lay one's memory down beside it.
And as they walked away, the seed started to germinate.
Christ began to live.

RONALD DUNCAN
(1914–   )

Eve's First Prophecy

God who made the garden green
Made the apple tree to lean
And glitter in that shine and sheen.

The apple tree will fall away.

Straight of bole and strict of bough,
Sons of mine will shape and hew
Tree that Eden never knew.

The dry tree branch will swing and sway.

All to this my sons are born:
To hew and shape and raise that tree,
And stand beneath in scorn, in scorn. . . .

The apple tree shall fall away.
The dry tree branch shall swing and sway.

ARCHIBALD MACLEISH
(1892–   )

Man Carries Woman

Man carries woman a way of the Cross,
Through thorns he must make it good;
With shoulders squared to the heavy weight,
He carries with his own blood:
Carries her suffering step by step,
And does it with hero mood.

He toils with the old ancestral urge
That spreads along through his blood
And roots down deep in his mind and heart
With the glow of its secret flood;
His way is like that to Golgotha,
The thorny way of the Rood.

And heavy upon the cross on high,
While he struggles on beneath,
Is the mighty war between soul and flesh;
He strains at his bonds with their galling mesh
And reddens his victory wreath.

Tore Örjasaeter
(1886–   )
Translated from the Norwegian by
Charles W. Stork

She Who Understands

Her dark head fallen forward in grief,
A beautiful woman, past her first youth,
Throws herself on her knees while an agonizing Christ
From the hard rood looks down in compassion.

Her eyes are charged with a burden of sorrow,
And her womb with a child to be born.
At the feet of the white Christ bleeding, she prays,
"Lord, do not let my child be born a woman."

ALFONSINA STORNI
(1892–1938)
*Translated from the Spanish by
Sister Maria Luisa, C.S.C.*

Debtors
From Kristin Lavransdatter

None, no, none of her children had [Kristin] loved as she loved this little child of sorrow. . . . She *could* not lose this child—and she could not save it—

Almighty God, Queen of Mercy, Holy Olav—she felt herself this time it availed not that she threw herself down and begged for the life of the child—

Forgive us our trespasses, as we forgive them that trespass against us—

She went to church each Mass-day as she was wont to do. She kissed the doorpost, sprinkled herself with holy water, bent her knee before the ancient crucifix above the choir arch. The Saviour looked down, sorrowful and gentle, in the anguish of death. Christ died to save His murderers. Holy Olav stands before His face, in everlasting supplication for the folk that drove him into outlawry and slew him—

As we forgive them that trespass against us.

Blessed Mary—my child dies! Know you not, Kristin, rather had I borne His cross and suffered His death than have stood under my Son's cross and seen Him die—But, since I knew that this must be, for the salvation of sinners, I gave consent in my heart—I gave consent when my Son prayed: Father, forgive them, for they know not what they do—

—As we forgive them that trespass against us—

The cry of your heart is no prayer until you have said your Paternoster without guile—

SIGRID UNDSET
(1882–1949)

The Rejection of Miracles

When man rejects miracles he rejects God too; for man seeks not so much God as the miraculous. And as man cannot bear to be without the miraculous, he will create new miracles of his own for himself, and will worship deeds of sorcery and witchcraft, though he might be a hundred times over a rebel, heretic and infidel. Thou didst not come down from the Cross when they shouted to Thee, mocking and reviling Thee: "Come down from the cross and we will believe that Thou art He." Thou didst not come down, for again Thou wouldst not enslave man by a miracle, and didst crave faith given freely, not based on miracles.

FYODOR DOSTOEVSKY
(1821–1881)

Now We Can Ease Our Minds

"Jesus grew up and raised the dead," [Lucette[1]] cried, "and the world shouted, 'Leave the dead lie. The dead are dead and can stay that way. What do we want with the dead alive?' Oh you people!" she shouted, "they nailed Him to a cross and run a spear through His side and then they said, 'Now we can have some peace, now we can ease our minds.' And they hadn't but only said it when they wanted Him to come again. Their eyes were opened and they saw the glory they had killed.

"Listen world," she cried, flinging up her arms so that the cape flew out behind her, "Jesus is coming again! The mountains are going to lie down like hounds at His feet, the stars are going to perch on His shoulder and when He calls it, the sun is going to fall like a goose for His feast. Will you know the Lord Jesus then? The mountains will know Him and bound forward, the stars will light on His head, the sun will drop down at His feet, but will you know the Lord Jesus then? . . .

"If you don't know Him now, you won't know Him then. Listen to me, world, listen to this warning. The Holy Word is in my mouth!"

FLANNERY O'CONNOR
(1925–1964)

⟨⟨⟨⟨⟨⟨⟨⟨⟨⟨⟨⟩

The Coronet

When for the thorns with which I long, too long,
   With many a piercing wound,
   My Saviour's head have crowned,
I seek with garlands to redress that wrong;

[1] In *The Violent Bear It Away,* Lucette is a precocious child-preacher, eleven or twelve years old.

Through every garden, every mead,
I gather flowers (my fruits are only flowers)
   Dismantling all the fragrant towers[1]
That once adorned my shepherdess's head.
And now when I have summed up all my store,
   Thinking (so I myself deceive)
   So rich a chaplet thence to weave
As never yet the king of glory wore;
   Alas I find the serpent old
   That, twining in his speckled breast,
   About the flowers disguised does fold,
   With wreaths of fame and interest.
Ah, foolish man, that wouldst debase with them,
And mortal glory, heaven's diadem!
   But Thou who only couldst the serpent tame,
Either his slippery knots at once untie,
And disentangle all his winding snare;
Or shatter too with him my curious frame,[2]
And let these wither, so that he may die,
Though set with skill and chosen out with care,
That they, while Thou on both their spoils dost tread,
May crown Thy feet, that could not crown Thy head.

ANDREW MARVELL
(1621–1678)

❦❦❦❦❦❦❦❦❦❦❦❦

A Hymn to God the Father

Hear me, O God!
A broken heart
Is my best part:

---

[1] Elaborate headdresses for ladies.
[2] The floral frame designed by the poet.

Use still thy rod,
    That I may prove
    Therein, thy love.

If thou hadst not
    Been stern to me,
    But left me free,
I had forgot
    My self and thee.

For, sin's so sweet,
    As minds ill bent
    Rarely repent,
Until they meet
    Their punishment.

Who more can crave
    Than thou hast done?
    That gav'st a Son
To free a slave:
    First made of nought;
    With all since bought.

Sin, death, and hell
    His glorious name
    Quite overcame;
Yet I rebel,
    And slight the same.

But I'll come in
   Before my loss
Me farther toss,
   As sure to win
      Under His cross.

BEN JONSON
(1573?–1637)

VII

THE GLORY TREE

Full oft I took thought   of the Tree of glory
Not once alone,   ere I learned the truth
Of the radiant Cross.

From *The Christ*, CYNEWULF

(died 785)

Were He not Thy Son   unsoiled of evil. . .
never, O Lord,
Wouldst thou have roused Him,   Ruler of nations,
In splendour from death   in the sight of men.

IBID.

Speak, Mary, declaring what you saw wayfaring:
"The tomb of Christ, who is living, the glory
of Jesus' resurrection."

SEQUENCE FOR EASTER, ROMAN MISSAL

SPLENDOR

On the first day of the week, at early dawn, they came to the tomb, taking the spices that they had prepared, and they found the stone rolled back from the tomb. But on entering, they did not find the body of the Lord Jesus. And it came to pass, while they were wondering what to make of this, that, behold two men stood by them in dazzling raiment. And when the women were struck with fear and bowed their faces to the ground, they said to them, "Why do you seek the living one among the dead? He is not here, but has risen. Remember how he spoke to you while he was yet in Galilee, saying that the Son of Man must be betrayed into the hands of sinful men, and be crucified, and on the third day rise." And they remembered his words.[1]

But Mary was standing outside weeping at the tomb. So, as she wept, she stooped down and looked into the tomb, and saw two angels in white sitting, one at the head and one at the feet, where the body of Jesus had been laid. They said to her, "Woman, why art thou weeping?" She said to them, "Because they have taken away my Lord, and I do not know where they have laid him."

When she had said this she turned round and beheld Jesus standing there, and she did not know that it was Jesus. Jesus said to her, "Woman, why art thou weeping? Whom dost thou seek?" She, thinking that it was the gardener, said to him, "Sir, if thou hast removed him, tell me where thou hast laid him and I will take him away." Jesus said to her, "Mary!" Turning, she said to him, "Rabboni!" (that is to say, Master). . . .[2]

---

[1] Luke xxiv.3-8.   [2] John xx.11-16.

After this he was manifested in another form to two of them, as they were walking on their way into the country. "What words are these that you are exchanging as you walk and are sad?"

But one of them, named Cleophas, answered and said to him, "Art thou the only stranger in Jerusalem who does not know the things that have happened there in these days?" And he said to them, "What things?"

And they said to him, "Concerning Jesus of Nazareth, who was a prophet, mighty in work and word before God and all the people; and how our chief priests and rulers delivered him up to be sentenced to death, and crucified him. But we were hoping that it was he who should redeem Israel. Yes, and besides all this, today is the third day since these things came to pass. And moreover, certain women of our company who were at the tomb before it was light, astounded us, and not finding his body, they came, saying that they had also seen a vision of angels, who said that he is alive. So some of our company went to the tomb, and found it even as the women had said, but him they did not see."

But he said to them, "O foolish ones and slow of heart to believe in all that the prophets have spoken! Did not the Christ have to suffer these things before entering into his glory?" . . .[3]

---

[3] Mark xvi.12-26.

Quem Quaeritis?
(Poem for Voices)

Whom do you seek? No life is in this ground.
The napkin stained and linen clothes lie round.
Here is no fountain but a land of dearth
Where thorns forget the forehead they had crowned.
Whom do you seek?

'What is pure gold or what are diamonds worth
To that first vision, men like trees on earth
Walking? For so He showed them first, and then
Opened my eyelids, who was blind from birth.'
Whom do you seek?

'In that clear stream I also was made clean.
Going from the priest, I turned, the last of ten,
To give God praise, being healed of leprosy,
Though He had warned me: Hide your praise from men.'
Whom do you seek?

'I was so hidden, my hand He could not see
When, in that press of people, on my knee
I touched His garment; yet my life was known.
That moment from affliction I went free.'
Whom do you seek?

'When, among graves, despairing I was thrown
By devils to the ground, I heard each stone
Echo His words, until the walls cried out:
Come out of him, and leave My son alone.'
Whom do you seek?

'He loosed my tongue. That power how could I doubt?
Though all denied Him, each would stay devout,
Had he been bound like me, both deaf and dumb,
Until those sudden fingers made me shout.'
Whom do you seek?

'They look for glory in day, and we in gloom.
We look for Him who has overcome the tomb.
By Him, by His first promise we are bound,
Whose narrow dwelling gives us greatest room.'
Whom do you seek?

VERNON WATKINS
(1906–   )

Easter: The Challenge to Death

If the Lord had not risen living from the tomb; if Mary had not
recognized Him in the Garden; if He had not manifested Himself
to Cephas; if He had not walked at twilight on a road with two
disciples as far as the inn where He heard the sweetest words that
humanity has ever addressed to Him, "Stay with us, for it is
getting towards evening, and the day is now far spent . . ."; if
St. Thomas had not placed his fingers in His wounds which no
longer bled; if Christ had not manifested Himself to more than
five hundred brethren, the majority of whom were still living when
Paul wrote his first Epistle to the Corinthians; and if Paul himself had not been dazzled and thrown to the ground at a turn in
the road, less by the blinding light than by the unendurable sweetness of this name, "I am Jesus, whom thou art persecuting"—
if all this history were not history, we would not this morning

be an innumerable throng around the empty tomb wherein our hope reposes.

It is precisely because in our eyes there exists no fact more certain and to which more people have borne witness than the Resurrection, that we find it repugnant to look for only a symbol in it, as do those of little faith, in whose eyes things have never transpired as the witnesses have reported.

Nevertheless there is no trait of this life of Christ that is not reflected in ours, miserable as they may be. . . . We are forbidden to be dead persons, we are solemnly enjoined to become living persons again.

FRANÇOIS MAURIAC
(1885–   )

Easter Hymn

Death and darkness get you packing,
Nothing now to man is lacking,
All your triumphs now are ended,
And what Adam marr'd, is mended;
Graves are beds now for the weary,
Death a nap, to wake more merry;
Youth now, full of pious duty,
Seeks in thee for perfect beauty,
The weak, and aged tir'd, with length
Of days, from thee look for new strength,
And infants with thy pangs contest
As pleasant, as if with the breast;
    Then, unto him, who thus hath thrown
Even to contempt thy kingdom down,

And by his blood did us advance
Unto his own inheritance,
To him be glory, power, praise,
From this, unto the last of days.

HENRY VAUGHAN
(1622–1695)

First Fruits

We were all dead, sayeth the Apostle; dead sheaves, all. One, and that is Christ, this day, the day of the first fruits, was in manner of a sheaf, taken out of the number of the dead, and in the name of the rest, lifted up from the graves, and in His rising, He shook, for there was a great earthquake. By virtue whereof, the first fruits being restored to life, all the rest of the dead are in Him entitled to the same hope, in that He was not so lifted up for himself alone, but for us and in our names: and so the substance of this feast [is] fulfilled in Christ's resurrection.

LANCELOT ANDREWES
(1555–1626)

O Felix Culpa!

So great a Saviour is ours; for his sake we were made, by his merits we have been redeemed. He died for us all, who had all become dead men; his mercy was the antidote to Adam's misery—ransoming the human race, rather than ruining it. So far was Adam's sin from getting the better of God's goodnaturedness, it stimulated, it inflamed it. The kindness of God, reacting gently and lovingly to human opposition, intervened to overcome it: as our fault was amplified, grace has been more amply bestowed than ever.[1] So that holy Church, in an ecstasy of wonderment, cries out at the Easter vigil: "O truly necessary sin of Adam, which Christ's death blotted out; and happy fault, that merited such a redeemer!" Most assuredly, we can echo that ancient Greek: "Had we not been lost, we were lost indeed."[2] In other words, our loss proved to be our gain—human nature, to be sure, received more grace through being redeemed by its Saviour than ever it would have received from Adam's unsullied innocence.

SAINT FRANCIS DE SALES
(1567–1622)

Easter

I

And I heard a great voice in the night, it was like the breath of the
    world, and cried: "Who will bear the Saviour's crown?"
And my love spoke: "Lord, I will bear it."
And I carried the crown in my hands, and from the black thorn the
    blood flowed down over my fingers.
But the voice cried again: "You must wear the crown on your
    head."
And my love answered: "Yes, I will wear it."
And I lifted the crown to my forehead, then a light broke from it,
    white as mountain waters.

---

[1] Rom. v.20.
[2] Themistocles.

And the voice cried: "Lo, the black thorn has blossomed!"

And the light ran down from my head and grew broad like a
stream and fell on my feet.

And I cried in great terror: "Lord, to what place shall I carry the
crown?"

And the voice answered: "You shall carry it into everlasting Life."

Then I said: "Lord, it is a crown of suffering, let me die of it."

But the voice spoke: "Know you not that suffering is immortal?
I have transfigured the Infinite: Christ is risen!"

Then the light swept me away.—

I I

And your voice speaks: I take the shoes from my feet, I put off all
that is finite and tread on a land without borders.

Burst forth, all the dark well-springs of my life!

Come flying all my nights, dark birds of guilt, descend upon me
with outstretched wings:

I will go into deepest sorrow that I may find my God.

For sorrow is great in the world, mighty and without end.

It has encompassed that against which heaven and earth are shattered, it has endured the weight of infinite love.

Holy God, Holy Strength, Holy Immortal,

Thou God under my sin, Thou God under my weakness, Thou
God under my death.

I lay my lips upon Thy wounds—Lord, I lay my soul upon Thy
cross.

GERTRUDE VON LE FORT
(1876–   )
*Translated from the German by
Margaret Chanler*

The Triumphal Alleluia

I

We are proclaiming your death, Lord;
we praise you, Christ, for your holy resurrection.
It is fitting, you say, for us to approach the table
of these ineffable mysteries.
Let us be eager, then, to receive our share
of the spiritual gifts here spread before us;
let us sing with the angels
the triumphal Alleluia.

God the Word, he in the Father's bosom,
was lately here upon the cross as well.
He was laid in a tomb like any mortal
—stooped so low, would have it so;
but on the third day rose again and gave us
O what gift of mercy.

ANONYMOUS, GREEK
(3rd to 6th century)

The Archvictor

It is clear that it is Christ Himself and none other Who is the
Archvictor over death and has robbed it of its power. Death used
to be strong and terrible, but now, since the sojourn of the Saviour
and the death and resurrection of His body, it is despised; and

obviously it is by the very Christ Who mounted on the Cross that
it has been destroyed and vanquished finally. When the sun rises
after the night and the whole world is lit up by it, nobody doubts
that it is the sun which has thus shed its light everywhere and
driven away the dark. Equally clear is it, since this utter scorning
and trampling down of death has ensued upon the Saviour's mani-
festation in the body and His death on the Cross, that it is He
Himself Who brought death to nought and daily raises monu-
ments to His victory in His own disciples. How can you think
otherwise, when you see men naturally weak hastening to death,
unafraid at the prospect of corruption, fearless of the descent
into Hades, even indeed with eager soul provoking it, not shrinking from tortures, but preferring thus to rush on death for Christ's
sake, rather than to remain in this present life? If you see with
your own eyes men and women and children, even, thus welcom-
ing death for the sake of Christ's religion, how can you be so
utterly . . . incredulous and maimed in your mind as not to realize
that Christ, to Whom these all bear witness, Himself gives victory to each, making death completely powerless for those who
hold His faith and bear the sign of the Cross? No one in his senses
doubts that a snake is dead when he sees it trampled underfoot,
especially when he knows how savage it used to be; nor, if he sees
boys making fun of a lion, does he doubt that the [animal] is
either dead or completely bereft of strength. These things can be
seen with our own eyes, and it is the same with the conquest of
death. Doubt no longer, then, when you see death mocked and
scorned by those who believe in Christ, that by Christ death was
destroyed, and the corruption that goes with it resolved and
brought to end.

SAINT ATHANASIUS
(293?–373)

Magdalen Speaks

He has appeared to me
as a gardener.
Sorrowful I was
and weeping, for I did not know
where I should find him.
And I came here seeking him.
When I turned I saw him behind me.
He asked me
why I was weeping;
but when I would have touched him,
he said, "Touch me not. . . ."

To him be praise!
Let him be served,
for he rooted up my sins
to plant me among the flowers.
Let us love him;
let us honor his holy temple;
let sinners trust in his help and his graces,
for I am an example unto them.

JUAN DEL ENCINA
(1468–1534)
Translated from the Spanish by
Sister M. Katharine Elaine, C.S.C.

Easter

Rise, heart, thy Lord is risen; sing His praise
    Without delays,
Who takes thee by the hand, that thou likewise
    With Him mayst rise;
That, as His death calcinèd thee to dust,
His life may make thee gold, and, much more, just.

Awake, my lute, and struggle for thy part
    With all thy art;
The cross taught all wood to resound His name
    Who bore the same;
His stretched sinews taught all strings what key
Is best to celebrate this most high day.

Consort both heart and lute, and twist a song
    Pleasant and long;
Or, since all music is but three parts vied
    And multiplied,
O, let Thy blessed spirit bear a part,
And make up our defects with His sweet art.

I got me flowers to straw Thy way;
I got me boughs off many a tree:
But Thou wast up by break of day,
And brought'st Thy sweets along with Thee.

The sun arising in the east,
Though he give light, and the east perfume,
If they should offer to contest
With Thy arising, they presume.

Can there be any day but this,
Though many suns to shine endeavor?
We count three hundred, but we miss:
There is but one, and that one ever.

GEORGE HERBERT
(1593–1633)

The Veteran of Heaven

O Captain of the wars, whence won Ye so great scars?
   In what fight did Ye smite, and what manner was the foe?
Was it on a day of rout they compassed Thee about,
   Or gat Ye these adornings when Ye wrought their overthrow?

' 'Twas on a day of rout they girded Me about,
   They wounded all My brow, and they smote Me through the
     side:
My hand held no sword when I met their armèd horde,
   And the conqueror fell down, and the Conquered bruised his
     pride.'

What is this, unheard before, that the Unarmed make war,
   And the Slain hath the gain, and the Victor hath the rout?
What wars, then, are these, and what the enemies,
   Strange Chief, with the scars of Thy conquest trenched about?

'The Prince I drave forth held the Mount of the North,
   Girt with the guards of flame that roll round the pole.
I drave him with My wars from all his fortress-stars,
   And the sea of death divided that My march might strike its
     goal.

'In the keep of Northern Guard, many a great dæmonian sword
  Burns as it turns round the Mount occult, apart:
There is given him power and place still for some certain days,
  And his name would turn the Sun's blood back upon its heart.'

What is *Thy* Name? Oh, show!—'My Name ye may not know;
  'Tis a going forth with banners, and a baring of much swords:
But My titles that are high, are they not upon My thigh?
  "King of Kings!" are the words, "Lord of Lords!";
  It is written "King of Kings, Lord of Lords." '

FRANCIS THOMPSON
(1859–1907)

Thomas and the Master

[Thomas] said: "Unless I touch Him, unless I put my finger in, I shall not believe." "Come, touch Me. Put in your finger and be not unbelieving but believing. Come, put in your finger. I knew your wounds. I have kept My wounds for you." Moreover, putting in his hand certainly confirmed the faith of that disciple. For what is the fullness of faith? That Christ be believed to be not merely Man, that Christ be believed to be not only God, but that He be believed to be both Man and God—that is the fullness of faith because "the Word was made flesh, and dwelt among us."

Therefore, when the wounds and limbs of His Saviour had been presented to him to be touched, the disciple touched them and exclaimed: "My Lord and my God!" He touched a Man; he recognized God. He touched flesh; he looked upon the Word, because "the Word was made flesh, and dwelt among us." This Word suffered His flesh to be hung upon a tree; this Word suffered His flesh to be fastened with nails; this Word suffered His flesh to be pierced with a lance; this Word suffered His flesh to be placed in a tomb; this Word raised His flesh to life, presented it to the gaze of His disciples, offered it to be touched by their hands. They touch and they cry out: "My Lord and my God!" This is the Day which the Lord hath made.

SAINT AUGUSTINE
(354–430)

The Road to Emmaus

Now has the third day's red sail come
To haven on its westering way;
In the soul—Golgotha, the tomb,
Dispute, and riot, and dismay.

And craftily, the cruel night
Stands everywhere on sentinel,
And though the warming sun is bright,
It has not strength the dark to quell.

Death, the inexorable, gapes;
The heart is stifled in the grave . . .
Somewhere are white and shining shapes,
Gold on the gloom, wrath on the wave!

And frenzied women, pale with tears,
Proclaim good tidings—but of what?
From crushing and denying fears
The lulling mist lets nothing out.

Someone, a stranger, on the road,
Stopping to speak to us, proclaims
A sacrificed and a dead God . . .
And the heart breathes again, and flames.

VYACHESLAV IVANOV
(1866–1949)
Translated from the Russian by
C. M. Bowra

Believe

From *Resurrexit*

That delicate honeycomb Christ took to mouth,
that plundered nest was sweet, to lips grown grey
with Judas kiss and gall. Not since Mary's milk
had ever the earth offered in cup or lip
such word as the shifty bees, this way and that
    stealing,
assuring: the dead flower lives: even death serves.

The dismembered fish too,
ikthus for Christ, stared up at the fearful
fishermen. They tossed unseaworthy
when the walker of waves stood there, and the floor
pitched them green. When he had eaten away all
but literal arrangement, the skeleton said
Jesus Christ, Son of God, Savior.[1]

---

[1] Because the letters of the Greek *ikthus* (fish) are composed of the initial
letters of Jesus Christ, Son of God, Saviour, the fish was used as a secret
symbol of the Eucharist in the catacombs.

Death again: the eyes
even of a dead fish crying: believe or drown.

DANIEL BERRIGAN
(1921–   )

Wood Against Wood

He laid wood against wood, and hands against hands: His generously extended hands against those that reach out with greed; His nail-pierced hands against those that are fallen in discouragement; His hands that embrace the whole world against the hand that brought about Adam's banishment from Paradise.

Yesterday I hung on the Cross with Christ; today I am glorified with Him; yesterday I was dying with Him, today I am brought to life with Him; yesterday I was buried with Him, today I rise with Him.

Let us become like Christ, since Christ also became like us. Let us become gods for Him, since He became man for us.

SAINT GREGORY OF NYSSA
(died *c.* 394)

Cross and Resurrection

Out of the fulness of his victory the Son gives each individual a special kind of participation in his passion on earth and in the profound mystery of judgment accomplished on Calvary. The participation granted in virtue of his victory may, by the will of the Lord, reach the point of an extreme powerlessness, an experience of inner darkness, abandonment and reprobation; and because it is a sharing in the cross, it surpasses anything naturally experienced and endured, even to the complete loss, subjectively, of all spiritual light, of any view or hope of a future redemption and resurrection. Yet this darkness most certainly proceeds from that light and presupposes it objectively, even subjectively, for the light is never withdrawn from any believer without his knowing it beforehand and his giving his consent to that loss, at least implicitly.

Thus the contemplation of the cross is comprised within that of the resurrection (for all faith is faith in the resurrection), and, further, in the contemplation of the cross the contemplation of one's own and the world's sins finds its true place.

HANS URS VON BALTHASAR
(1905-   )

Most Glorious Lord of Lyfe

Most glorious Lord of lyfe, that on this day,
Didst make thy triumph over death and sin:
And having harrowd hell, didst bring away
Captivity thence captive us to win:
This joyous day, deare Lord, with joy begin,
And grant that we for whom thou diddest dye
Being with thy deare blood clene washt from sin,
May live for ever in felicity.
And that thy love we weighing worthily,
May likewise love thee for the same againe:

And for thy sake that all lyfe deare didst buy,
With love may one another entertayne.
So let us love, deare love, lyke as we ought,
Love is the lesson which the Lord us taught.

EDMUND SPENSER
(1552–1599)

Michael the Archangel to Adam
From Paradise Lost

                           Death over him no power
Shall long usurp; ere the third dawning light
Return, the stars of morn shall see him rise
Out of his grave, fresh as the dawning light,
Thy ransom paid, which man from death redeems,
His death for Man, as many as offer'd life
Neglect not, and the benefit embrace
By faith not void of works: this God-like act
Annuls thy doom, the death thou shouldst have di'd,
In sin for ever lost from life; this act
Shall bruise the head of Satan, crush his strength
Defeating Sin and Death, his two main arms,
And fix far deeper in his head their stings
Than temporal death shall bruise the Victor's heel,
Or theirs whom he redeems, a death like sleep,
A gentle wafting to immortal life.
Nor after resurrection shall he stay
Longer on earth than certain times to appear
To his disciples, men who in his life
Still follow'd him; to them shall leave in charge
To teach all nations what of him they learn'd

And this salvation, them who shall believe
Baptizing in the profluent stream, the sign
Of washing them from guilt of sin to life
Pure, and in mind prepar'd, if so befall,
For death, like that which the redeemer di'd.

JOHN MILTON
(1608–1674)

Humanity Transfigured

For many minds, the Resurrection of Christ represents the point at which they stop short. Up to the time of His Passion Christ is a historical figure. From the Resurrection onward, He belongs to the realm of faith. And it is true that the Resurrection is indeed a dividing line. Up to the time of His burial, the life of Christ is unfolded on the level of ordinary human existence. From the time of the Resurrection, He enters a different order, that of trans-figured humanity. But it remains true that this contrast is much less important than it appears at first sight. . . . From its outset the life of Christ belonged to the domain of the mighty works of God. Already we were deep in mystery. And if that life was un-folded on the level of ordinary human existence, this does not mean that that existence represented a natural order as opposed to a supernatural world. It was already related to a supernatural world, that of human nature in its state of misery and corruptibility. In that He was made flesh, the Word of God was accessible to carnal man. But this carnal condition is only one of the states of humanity, that of its fall.

When we come to the Resurrection, the opposite is true. The Word of God withdraws His Manhood from the carnal condition, and thus conceals it from the gaze of carnal man. But as it is that same Manhood which exists first of all in the conditions of the flesh, and now exists in the conditions of the spirit, it is clear that this transition is bound to have a "footprint" in the world of the flesh. This footprint, this symbol, is the empty tomb. It is a negative symbol, which in no way enables us to grasp the essential content of the Resurrection, for that is inaccessible to the flesh, and no historian or philosopher will ever encounter it in the course of applying his own technique. But this negative symbol is highly important, inasmuch as it encompasses the empty space wherein the Resurrection takes place, and sets its very locality within the pattern of ordinary history.

This is the very reason why it undoubtedly constitutes the fact which those who seek to separate the Jesus of history from the Jesus of faith are most often forced to reject. Already the Jews had spread the rumour that the disciples had stolen the body of Christ, which is perhaps the most valuable evidence for the existence of the open tomb. Later the very reality of the fact was to be challenged, or its whole meaning was to be denied. It is more convenient, indeed, to dissociate the two levels entirely from one another, and to protect the Christ of faith by detaching Him completely from the results of historical criticism. But the empty tomb is just what prevents us from placing the heavenly story of the Word side by side with the earthly story of Jesus, and thus compels us to recognize that the Word has really come in the flesh, and that the flesh in its turn is really quickened by the Word. So we are obliged to maintain the rigorous continuity of the Jesus of history with the Jesus of faith, but seeing them simply as two states of the single Manhood of Jesus.

But if it is an integral part of Christ's Manhood, the Resurrection is equally an integral part of the continuity of the works which the Trinity performs in and through the Manhood of Christ. The Resurrection may even be called the supremely divine work, because it is strictly the divinization of man by the virtue of the Spirit. It is not only a reanimation, which would be merely a return to and a prolonging of mortal life, even if that life were to be prolonged indefinitely. But it is the passing from one mode of existence to another. The death from which it frees the Manhood of Christ is not only the separation of soul and body, but the mortal condition as such, of which the separation of soul and body is only the final expression. And the life which it communicates is not the state of man while his soul animates his body; it is the life of God grasping the soul and body, removing them from the misery of the flesh and communicating to them the glory of the Spirit.

It is in the Resurrection that the condition of man as it is present in the eternal design of God is brought to fulfilment. For God created man for incorruptibility. From the beginning He set man in Paradise, that is, in the midst of divinizing energies. It is sin that reduced man to the condition of the flesh by separating him from the life of God. In Christ once more, and this time for ever, mankind is quickened by the life of the Spirit. This is accomplished first and foremost in the Manhood of Christ, in order that it may be the instrument by which that life may be communicated to the rest of mankind. "His was the first birth out of death; thus in every way the primacy was to become his."

JEAN DANIÉLOU
(1905–   )

Easter Hymn

If in that Syrian garden, ages slain,
You sleep, and know not you are dead in vain,
Nor even in dreams behold how dark and bright
Ascends in smoke and fire by day and night

The hate you died to quench and could but fan,
Sleep well and see no morning, son of man.

But if, the grave rent and the stone rolled by,
At the right hand of majesty on high
You sit, and sitting so remember yet
Your tears, your agony and bloody sweat,
Your cross and passion and the life you gave,
Bow hither out of heaven and see and save.

A. E. HOUSMAN
(1859–1936)

Easter Sunday

Last night did Christ the Sun rise from the dark,
    The mystic harvest of the fields of God,
And now the little wandering tribes of bees
    Are brawling in the scarlet flowers abroad.
The winds are soft with birdsong; all night long
    Darkling the nightingale her descant told,
And now inside church doors the happy folk
    The Alleluia chant a hundredfold.
O father of thy folk, be thine by right
The Easter joy, the threshold of the light.

SEDULIUS SCOTTUS
(*flourished* 848–874)
Translated from the Latin by
Helen Waddell

The Eternal Immolation of the Lamb

We might say that Easter is the Christian Sinai, and that the dead and risen Christ is the table of the new law, except that Easter is more than the voice of God upon the mountain and Christ greater than any table of law. But Easter is the bursting forth of the holiness of the Spirit of God in a man, Christ, and the transformation of that man into the holiness of the Spirit of God, and our progressive transformation into that man. Such is Christian morality: the mystery of Christ dead to the flesh in the divine life of the Holy Spirit, growing ever stronger in us. . . .

Heavenly love is the marriage feast, a feast at the foot of the Cross, begun in the last eucharistic supper; all are united in the immolated body of Christ, and in that body are united to each other. The indestructible society, which every sacrificial meal has aimed at bringing about, is now perfected.

Thus God is all in all, as it is his nature to be; he impresses upon all, in the Holy Ghost, his form of life, which is love.

The centre from which this living love radiates is the Lamb, the paschal victim. The end of a study of Christ's glorification will bring our minds back to his death and fix them there. For that is where his glory began, and still begins, even in heaven. The Lamb stands slain (Apoc. v.6), and the faithful, in turn, triumph only in death—their death which is Christ's death communicated to them. The glory is marked by the stigmata of his five wounds. The immolation remains inscribed in it, not as a memory, but as a reality, and proclaims for all eternity the death the Lamb submitted to for love of his Father.

He came down to live in the world of sin and slavery, in order that that world might receive a mortal blow in his body. He left the world below and entered heaven through the wounding of his body. But he has left his body, slain and brought back to life, among men, to be the living way along which they can go to the Father. In him men take their departure, in him they attain their end. When that end is achieved all the sons will then have rejoined their Father. Honour and glory to the Lamb!

FRANCIS X. DURRWELL

(1912–   )

Twelve Thousand Signed

Thy great prophet tells in vision and in image, that he saw all those who took part in the first resurrection and that there were of each tribe twelve thousand. But if there were so many of them, they must have been not men but gods. They had borne Thy cross, they had endured scores of years in the barren, hungry wilderness, living upon locusts and roots—and Thou mayest indeed point with pride at those children of freedom, of free love, of free and splendid sacrifice for Thy name.

FYODOR DOSTOEVSKY

(1821–1881)

Easter Day

Let us lie still with our eyes closed a moment before dawn breaks on the day of the Resurrection. It is yet night, but already someone is stirring in two or three houses in Jerusalem. Lamps are being lit, and women are hurriedly dressing and combing their hair. The Sabbath is over, and one incomparable star irradiates the upturned face of our first Sunday. The shoemaker's cock prepares to take up the challenge flung at him by his friend on the other side of the Cedron. It is no longer Passover, it is Easter! Look, listen: in the Hebraic stillness there takes place, at the joining of three roads, a meeting of veiled women who exchange questions in hushed voices. "Who will roll the stone back from the entrance?" Who will take it away? The very fragrance they bear provides the answer. It is this irresistible quality of hope in their hearts, this emanation of mysterious ingredients prepared in the bosom of the night by the very hands of the dawn. Stored up for centuries, slowly expanding, this sacred chemistry which just now rose from sleep advances to triumph over death.

As for the remaining events of that wondrous morning, thanks to the bewildered and incoherent echo of the four interwoven Gospels, they reverberate to this day in every church in Christendom.

PAUL CLAUDEL
(1868–1955)

Girls Going to Church

Morning is Easter on the lawns,
And trim and flowered along the avenue
The girls go summering to church and season
Announced by heel-taps to the view.

Under the open window hats and ribbons
Declare for Spring *O find me, I am young*

Or, passing now, the sudden nervous giggle
Speaks on the light for Whom the hymn is sung.

See, see me, I am fair, and would arrive
Across the slant and stair of early light
To lord and lover. As grass many,
*   Or single as the night.*

. . . Because the year is stirring underfoot
Where choir-sung dryads from the Spring-flushed wood
Cry longing on the hush of Eucharist,
The bread and wine, the body and the blood.

JOHN CIARDI
(1916–   )

The Stair

Thursday, Friday, Sunday are the stair
You follow steadily in cold spring air.

On Thursday night the little company
Surrounding You as foliage its flower
Sees You arise and start toward Calvary
So to unfold uniquely in Your hour.

The Friday soldiers long ago portended,
Being a part of sorrow's royal day
On which the fiber of the world's new-stranded,
Raise You, unknowingly, upon Your way.

We follow tread by tread the steep short stair
Of Thursday, Friday, and of Sunday. There
We find You standing in the shriven air.

LOUISE TOWNSEND NICHOLL
(contemporary)

From Vision and Prayer

I turn the corner of prayer and burn
In a blessing of the sudden
Sun. In the name of the damned
I would turn back and run
To the hidden land
But the loud sun
Christens down
The sky.
I
Am found.
O let him
Scald me and drown
Me in his world's wound.
His lightning answers my
Cry. My voice burns in his hand.
Now I am lost in the blinding
One. The sun roars at the prayer's end.

DYLAN THOMAS
(1916–1953)

Epilogue
The Vision of the Cross in Paradise[1]

I understood that I had been raised up
by the burning smile of the star
more brilliantly red than ever before.

With all my heart, and in a tongue
the same for all men, I offered to God
a holocaust befitting this new grace.

The fervor of my sacrifice was not yet spent
when I knew it to be accepted by God
and sanctioned by Him wholly.

For, from out the splendor, two beams appeared
of such white-hot-rose brilliance that I cried out,
"O Helios, it is you who made them so beautiful!"

As the galaxy, agleam with greater and lesser lights
glows between the world's poles
so white it perplexes the wise,

So these constellated beams formed in the utmost depth
of Mars that adorable Sign which quadrants,
intersecting, make in the midst of a circle.[2]

---

[1] Editor's title; from *Il Paradiso*.
[2] The cross thus formed in a circle of light is a Greek cross, traditionally placed in the halo of Christ.

Here memory's strength overwhelms thought,
for on this cross of light Christ shone so glorious,
I can find no image to express Him.

But he who shoulders his cross and follows Him
will forgive my failure when in this glory
I saw Christ like lightning flash forth, sparkling.

From one arm of the cross to the other, from top to foot,
lights were running; where they joined or were crossing,
there they flamed the more.

Below on earth one also could see elements gathered
in particles, long, short, moving straight
or sinuous, fast or slow, all in a beam of light—

A beam like that defining light that sometimes edges shadows
wherein men contrive with art and skill
to protect themselves.

As lute and harp, their strings vibrating in harmony,
come in felicitous murmurs to those
who do not know the notes,

So here the lights came to me,
a melody spread on the Cross, a melody that enraptured
though I did not understand its words.

Like one who listens with hearing blurred, I hearkened.
A hymn of high praise I knew the song to be,
for it sang in my ears, "Arise!" and "Triumph!"

I was then so enraptured with love
that nothing before nor since that hour
has bound me with such sweet chains.

DANTE ALIGHIERI
(1265–1321)
Translated from the Italian by
Marusha Smilyanich

INDEX OF AUTHORS

About the Editor

SISTER MARY IMMACULATE is a Sister of the Congregation of the Holy Cross, and a professor of English at Saint Mary's College, Notre Dame, Indiana. She holds a B.A. from that institution, and a Ph.D. from Yale. She has contributed articles on medieval literature to scholarly periodicals, and poetry to various magazines. At present Sister is assembling materials for her second anthology.